BACKGROUND

BOOKS

JOHN LAFARGE

Gentle Jesuit

Father John LaFarge, S.J.

John LaFarge

GENTLE JESUIT

BY *Flora Strousse*

ILLUSTRATED BY SALEM TAMER

American
Background
Books

P. J. KENEDY & SONS · NEW YORK

FOR

FATHER HUGH J. NOLAN

scholar and friend

Books by the same author:
THE FRIAR AND THE KNIGHT
    Padre Olmedo and Cortez
MARGARET HAUGHERY
    Bread Woman of New Orleans
JOHN FITZGERALD KENNEDY
    Man of Courage
JOHN MILTON
THE LITTLEST CHRISTMAS TREE

ACKNOWLEDGMENT

Most of the information in this book was taken from Father LaFarge's own charming autobiography, *The Manner Is Ordinary*. His wisdom and wit made writing this work a pleasure. Further material was found in its sequel, *An American Amen*, and also in Father La-Farge's other works listed below.

F. S.

BOOKS BY JOHN LaFARGE

The Manner Is Ordinary   (1957)
A Report on the American Jesuits   (1956)
The Race Question and the Negro   (1943)
Interracial Justice   (1937)
A John LaFarge Reader   (1956)
The Catholic Viewpoint on Race Relations   (1956)
No Postponement   (1950)
The Jesuits in Modern Times   (1928)
An American Amen   (1958)

Contents

1.	The Nursery Stove	11
2.	Test of Faith	29
3.	Father Comes Home	44
4.	At Harvard	62
5.	Fateful Decision	78
6.	Young Jesuit	93
7.	The Ridge	108
8.	Interracial Justice	127
9.	The Ordinary Way	146
10.	God Had Chosen	163
11.	Love Unlimited	176
	Index	185
	About the Author	189

1

The Nursery Stove

HOME WAS A TWO-STORY FRAME HOUSE in Newport, Rhode Island. Until recently, this had seemed the center of the world to John LaFarge, the youngest of ten. He had never been so strong as the other children. So he had been petted by both his mother and his older brothers and sisters. Here he had always felt as safe as a caterpillar in a cocoon. Now, though, he was forced to try his wings, in school, and as predicted, he had been the brightest student in his class.

To bolster him up for this new venture, John's sister Emily had said, "I'm sure none of the other children could read when they were four."

His brother Bancel and his sister Margaret had agreed with Emily. The youngest member of their family, they were certain, would be far ahead of the other first-graders. John would bowl them over with all his "learning." His sister Frances, who loved to tease, had laughingly tossed in, "Before you know it, John will be teaching the class."

Oliver, handsome and fun-loving, had objected that too much fuss was being made about John's going to school. Everyone went to school when the time came. Of course John was bright, but there were other things in life besides studying, Oliver added. John should play more, make friends his own age, and be less serious.

And John had tried to follow this advice. Indeed, he already had made some friends. The closest were Perry and Walter Hill, whose mother "kept" the school he was attending. They and their sister Catherine were the first children of his own age John had ever known. They often played together both in and out of school. John was always welcome at the Hill's. He and Walter had become best friends.

One Friday after school, as the two boys sat chatting about this and that, Mr. Hill came home. He had left work early so that the family could go on a picnic at Easton's Point. When Mrs. Hill heard her husband's voice, she hurried from the kitchen.

"It will be so nice not to have to cook this evening," she said. She hugged her husband, and the children shouted with joy. And suddenly John knew the most important difference between his family and the Hills. *His* father didn't come home. He was always away on a trip somewhere with a friend named Henry

Adams, a famous writer. And now as John watched Mr. and Mrs. Hill, young and gay and loving one another, the boy felt lonely for a father.

Mrs. Hill asked John if he would like to join them on the picnic. Of course, he must first ask permission. John hesitated and then decided no. He felt too mixed up inside and wanted to think things out, but of course he couldn't explain that to Mrs. Hill.

Somehow, she seemed to read his mind, and knew that he was sad.

"Oh, well, we'll have another picnic soon," she said cheerfully, "and you can come along."

John wanted to thank her, but his voice seemed to be gone; so he merely nodded.

Then he noticed a sort of secret glance between the older Hills. Somehow it seemed to say that they were sorry for him, John thought. And all of a sudden he remembered other looks of pity that had been given to his mother. He remembered a snatch of conversation he had overheard:

"Poor Margaret LaFarge—she hasn't had much help bringing up all those children."

"Well, what can you expect? Artists are all the same."

It was hard for John to smile when he said, "I have to go—so long—be seeing you."

"Sure," Walter said. "Monday. Maybe sooner."

John rushed out of the house. Although he was usually a slow walker, his feet now flew. He must hurry home and comfort Mother. Hurry, hurry, down Ocean Drive, busy with plans for a gay social season. Here were the huge mansions of millionaires who had turned Newport from a sea-faring town into a famous summer resort. The boy moved even faster as he neared his own neighborhood. Most of the people here were bookish Boston folk called "intellectuals." Their families had settled there during the mid-nineteenth century. Now in the year 1886, most of these interesting people were friends of his own family.

As he rounded the end of Cliff Walk, John saw Miss Edith Wharton, a famous author, reclining in a chair on her veranda. Often she and the little boy had talks. Now, though, John merely waved and hurried on. A few doors from his own house, he spied another lady author. She was Miss Sarah Woolsey, who had written a series of books for young people called *What Katie Did.* Miss Woolsey was the tallest woman John had ever seen—like a giantess, almost —and John was amused that such a *big* person should write for *little* people.

Miss Woolsey turned—garden shears in hand—and

called out heartily, "Hi there, John. Want to stop by for lemonade and cookies?"

As a rule, he would have promptly accepted this invitation. Miss Woolsey seemed to know just how to converse with a boy, and she did bake such delicious cookies. He didn't stop now, but called back over his shoulder, "Sorry, I can't. I'm in a hurry," and sped on to his house.

As soon as John flung himself into the living room, he realized that his mother did not need comforting. She sat merrily chatting with a circle of LaFarges, her gaze fastened especially on her almost grown-up son Grant, who had arrived unannounced from college for the weekend. When John burst in upon the scene, his mother exclaimed, "Look who's here, John. Isn't this a wonderful surprise!"

Before John could react he received a friendly whack across the shoulders from his oldest brother.

"You're looking fine," Grant said. "And I do believe you've put on a few pounds. How goes it with our young scholar?"

John was pleased and embarrassed all at once. He didn't know quite what to say.

His sisters Margaret and Frances broke in, telling Grant all about how well John was doing in school. John's eye climbed to the tip of his brother's head.

It would be wonderful to be so tall and confident. Why, Grant must be as old as Mr. Hill! Indeed, all his brothers and sisters were more like grown-up relatives than childhood companions.

After a while, Bancel and Oliver, who had been out sailing, joined the family reunion. Soon, they were all discussing parties and plans for the week-end. And young John felt the way the tail of a kite must feel—not part of the whole, but a scraggly piece of rag tied on. The family loved him—this he knew. But somehow it didn't seem the same as the way Walter and Perry and Catherine Hill felt about one another. They had more fun *together*. He heard his mother's voice then.

"My, you're quiet, John," she said. "Don't you feel well?"

"I'm all right," John assured her.

At once, everyone began to pay attention to him. Grant showed John his watch, which was the most wonderful timepiece in the world. It chimed like the clock on the church steeple. After that Bancel asked if John would like to see his bird egg collection.

Would he! Excitement robbed him of his voice again, so he merely nodded.

Bancel produced a key to the small brass padlock of his lacquered cabinet. Inside were shallow drawers containing rows of birds' eggs embedded in cotton wool. Each had a neat label telling what kind of bird it belonged to. As John peered down on the delicate, multi-colored eggs, he thought they might become alive and warm and breathing. Then he remembered what he had read in the Bible. God cared for all his creation, even the "fallen robin." This thought made John feel better, and soon he was chatting merrily with the others.

Mother had prepared Grant's favorite dishes for supper that night. In the middle of dessert—which was Boston cream pie—Bancel suggested that the brothers go for a walk on the beach when they had finished eating. And John should come along. "You can watch the waves rise and fall in the moonlight," his brother added. "You always enjoy that."

Mother thought this was a fine idea. But before they left the table, she went on, she had something to tell the family. She had received a letter from their father that morning. Her husband had written that he and Mr. Adams had just returned from Japan.

John's heart beat a little faster, as he heard the news. Maybe now, his father would come home and they could all go on picnics like the Hills.

"When will Father be here?" his sister Margaret asked.

"Not for a while," their mother said. Then she explained that her husband had to remain in New York, where he had been commissioned to do an enormous painting of the Ascension in the Episcopal Church of the Ascension on Fifth Avenue. This news was followed by a disappointed silence. Then Oliver broke in: "He might have stopped to bid us the time of day. Father's been home so seldom these past years. I'll bet John doesn't even remember him."

Good as it was, the Boston cream pie seemed to stick in John's throat. His mother must have noticed.

"You mustn't feel badly, John," she said. "Your father asks about you in every letter. And he's delighted to hear what a good student you are."

Frances recalled that their father had come home more often when she was a little girl. This brought up memories of the time when the artist had his studio right here in Newport. How exciting that had been! . . . Still, they all agreed that a great artist like their father sometimes had to travel far in search of inspiration. And they realized that an artist also had to carry out his big commissions, like the mural painting for the Ascension Church in New York, right on the spot, not at home in Newport.

Maybe the others didn't mind about their father's absences, but young John did.

Now he was not only lonely for their father, but

confused as well. He did not understand all this grown-up talk about "inspiration" and "commissions." And that made him feel angry with everyone in general. So when Bancel told him to run upstairs and get a sweater, John said, "I don't want to go for a walk."

"Lazy bones," his sister Frances teased.

"If John has changed his mind, that's his privilege," Grant said. "He's not a child any more." With that he turned to the others and said, "Come on, fellows. Let's go before the moon moves on."

John felt even more "out of it" now. He went into the living room and watched his brothers down the sidewalk, while the gay chatter of his mother and sisters floated from the kitchen, where they were washing the dishes. Alone, seated in a large armchair, he gazed gloomily about, feeling sorry for himself.

Of the whole big house, this was the room he usually enjoyed the most. Each nook and corner was alive with treasures. Some of these he was not allowed to touch—or at least had to handle gently. One was the *cloisonné* matchbox on the gray marble mantelpiece. Then, too, he had to take care not to topple over a statue of the Child Jesus that stood on the staircase post. On the walls hung portraits of his mother and Bancel and his brother, Raymond, who had died. All of these had been painted by his father.

These pictures really were beautiful, John admitted.

Perhaps he should be proud to have an artist-father. But he'd rather have one like Mr. Hill.

Shadows deepened in the living room and it was growing chilly. John thought it would be better if a fire were burning in the hearth. More than anything, he loved to watch flames flicker, dance, and leap. Although he was not permitted to—he would probably be punished—he decided to light up the logs. After moving back the screen, John stood on tiptoe, took the silver box from the mantel, and was about to strike a match, when a voice called from the kitchen.

"What are you doing, John?" Emily asked.

"Nothing."

She came to him, took away the box and said, "You know you're not supposed to strike a match."

John adored his oldest sister, Emily. Sometimes she seemed almost like a mother. She was the one who punished him when he misbehaved, usually by putting him in a large closet until he promised to be good. And John was always rewarded with a chocolate cigarette when he was released. This would probably happen now, he thought. Instead, Emily asked, "Is something bothering you, John?"

He burst into tears, but would not tell her why he was sad. But, Emily seemed to guess. After lighting the fire, she spoke about their father, and told John that he was a most unusual man. "In his own way, he loves us all," she explained. Then she put her hand on John's head. It was a little warm. Perhaps John was coming down with a cold; he had better go to bed.

Emily tucked the covers in, as she had always done when he was very young. Then she lighted a fire in the small iron "nursery" stove. After she left, John watched the flames flickering beneath the small panes of isinglass. They sent out shadowy patterns on the wall. Sometimes the shapes were like vines or flowers or even fish—like the rock bass his brothers caught off Brenton's Point.

This iron stove was special. It seemed to be John's very own. He often gazed through the little windows and asked himself what he would be when he grew up. Perhaps I shall be like Father Cronan, John thought. Father Cronan was assistant pastor in their church. He was kind—another sort of father. But he wouldn't be an artist, John now decided; artists have to leave their families too much. Still, other fathers had to leave their children, too. After all, many of the children who went to Mrs. Hill's school were sons and daughters of Navy officers, and their fathers were often away at sea.

With that new idea, John forgot his worries and fell asleep.

One day, as John returned home from school, his mother met him at the door to announce that they had visitors. One was his uncle, Thomas Sergeant Perry, professor of English at Harvard University. The other was Mr. Okakura Kakuzo, a Japanese friend of John's father. Mr. Okakura was to spend a few days with them, and John was warned that he should make their guest feel at home.

Filled with curiosity—for he had never seen a Japanese man—John went into the living room. There Uncle Thomas greeted him and then introduced him to the Oriental visitor, saying that he was a famous writer.

In spite of this distinction, Mr. Okakura rose and bowed politely from the waist. Young John did the same.

During his visit Mr. Okakura wore a colorful Japanese costume. He would sit on a stuffed parlor chair with his white stockinged feet tucked under him. Nearby, his straw sandals remained on the floor. He was the center of an admiring circle of LaFarges.

One morning John was fortunate enough to find their visitor alone in the living room. Mr. Okakura was sitting as still as a statue, and John decided that their guest must be deep in thought. Not wanting to intrude, he seated himself on a chair and waited in silence.

Before long, Mr. Okakura said, "Now we shall talk."

"Oh, I'd like that!" John blurted out.

"What would you like to discuss?" Mr. Okakura asked.

Pleased to be treated like a grown-up, John replied honestly, "I'd like to know what you think about the white race, sir."

Because John seemed a thoughtful boy, the visitor said, he would tell exactly how he felt in general about the white race. Actually, he believed that the white man had nothing much to boast of; in fact—and this he almost whispered—he considered some of their tastes and attitudes quite deplorable.

"Look at your homes," Mr. Okakura continued politely. "Your pictures are hung without regard of place or sequence or logic." The guest paused for a moment and then went on, "In Japan, a single *kakemono* hangs on the wall for the family to contemplate."

Although John was not certain what a *kakemono* was, he supposed it might be something like a shrine. He wasn't sure about "contemplate" either, but he guessed, and said, "To examine oneself is good for the soul."

"That," Mr. Okakura said, "is a very wise remark." Then he went on to discuss other Western practices that bothered him.

"Take milk, for instance."

"Milk?" said John, in an amazed tone.

"Yes," the visitor went on. "Milk comes from the interior of a cow, and so do butter and cheese." The idea of eating such products made him positively ill, Mr. Okakura declared.

John found his face flushing with embarrassment. The LaFarge family consumed huge quantities of milk, and served it to their guests. Yet Mr. Okakura had shown no sign of being sick to his stomach at meals. This showed great self-control, thought John.

"What would you like to discuss?"
Mr. Okakura asked.

Because their talk had been confidential, John did
not mention Mr. Okakura's distaste for milk to his
mother. He himself, though, refrained from eating
dairy products for the rest of Mr. Okakura's visit.

During summer vacation John and his mother took a
trip to Jenkintown, Pennsylvania, a suburb of Phila-

delphia, to visit his Grandmother Perry. On the way
his mother explained that "Nonna"—which was what
the children called Grandmother Perry—might make
some slighting remarks about Catholics. John mustn't
mind if she did. None of the Perrys or the Sergeants—which was Nonna's family name—had ever
married Catholics. "My mother didn't approve of my
marriage," John's mother said.

When they arrived in Philadelphia, Mother and son
stopped off at church before they continued their journey to Jenkintown. As a Episcopalian, Nonna saw no
need for daily Mass; so the Catholic LaFarges might
not have another opportunity to "make a visit."

While kneeling beside his mother in the pew, John
prayed that Grandmother Perry would like him, even
though he was a Catholic.

As it turned out, Nonna seemed to like him very
much. Moreover, she claimed that this grandson fa-
vored her side of the family.

"I'm not so sure," John's mother said. "I think John
has his father's eyes."

"Nonsense!" Nonna snapped.

Then she talked about the past—of her happy girlhood and of her own father, Judge Thomas Sergeant,
who had been Justice of the Supreme Court of Pennsylvania.

"And I have a very important ancestor," Nonna

went on dreamily. "Benjamin Franklin. He was a statesman, printer, scientist, and writer, and he also helped to draft the Declaration of Independence."

John assured his grandmother that he knew about Benjamin Franklin. How he had tied a key to a string and flown his kite in a thunderstorm. "Lightning struck and that proved electricity," he added.

Nonna nodded, and then spoke of important people on her husband's side of the family, the Perrys. Her dear departed husband, she explained, was the son of Commodore Oliver Hazard Perry, a famous American naval officer.

"What did he do that made him famous?" young John asked.

Nonna told him almost as though she had been present at the scene.

During the War of 1812, this Commodore led his men to victory over the British in the Battle of Lake Erie. His words on that occasion had come down through history. They had been written in a message sent to Washington, Nonna told him. "We have met the enemy and they are ours," she quoted with patriotic passion.

"Oh, I've heard that," her grandson said in a flash of recognition, "but I didn't know he belonged to our family."

Nonna then turned to another Commodore Perry:

her husband's uncle, Matthew Calbraith Perry. If it hadn't been for Matthew Perry, she related, the East and West might never have met.

John tried to pay attention, but he was getting sleepy, and his mother suggested that he should take a nap. As he was dozing off, John wondered why people looked down on those different from themselves. He remembered what Mr. Okakura had said about the white race.

2

Test of Faith

WHEN JOHN'S grade-school years at Mrs. Hill's were over, he was sent to the red brick Coddington Public School on Mill Street. But he and Walter Hill remained closest friends. Although most of his schoolmates seemed to like him, John knew that some of the fellows considered him a "bookworm," and a "bust" when it came to sports.

In the class above him was a boy called Butch, who bulged all over with muscles. Some of the students thought Butch was great, but others secretly admitted he was nothing but a bully. John liked to make up his own mind about people and he hadn't yet formed an opinion. Occasionally he had seen Butch pick on a younger classmate, but he supposed that this was some people's idea of having fun. Actually, he didn't understand why boys found it amusing to fight and trip one another and play pranks and jokes on others. Still, his brother Oliver always remarked that John was far too

29

serious; so perhaps he wasn't the best judge of what was "fun."

Then one day at recess John saw a group of boys at the far end of the schoolyard. He decided to investigate. Within the circle Butch had a skinny, frightened boy pinned to the ground and was bending back his fingers.

"Say 'uncle,' " Butch commanded.

His captive, though obviously in pain, remained silent.

Butch pressed the fingers harder.

A few of the onlookers were urging Butch on, but most were disapprovingly silent.

John spoke up in his reasonable tone, and asked, "Why do you want him to say 'uncle'?"

Amazement broke Butch's hold. He wheeled around and shouted, "Who wants to know?"

"I do. Why should he particularly say 'uncle'?"

This was followed by hoots of scorn from Butch's friends.

Being upheld by his buddies was not enough for Butch. Slowly he advanced toward John, saying, "I'll button up your lip, you little mick."

John's curiosity was stronger than his fear. "What's a mick?" he asked innocently.

"An Irishman—a no-good, low-down Irishman,"

"Why do you want him to say 'uncle'?"

Butch said. After a moment's hesitation, he added, "All Catholics are micks."

Although Butch now towered threateningly above him, John thought he had better set the fellow straight. "You're mistaken about that," he said. "My father's family is French. My mother is a descendant of Benjamin Franklin and Commodore Perry."

This announcement caused Butch's fist to falter on its way.

Later, recalling the scene, John decided that Butch's fist would probably have landed on his nose if the gym instructor hadn't arrived at that moment. He ordered the boys to break it up and told Butch he had better stop picking on the smaller boys, or else he would be suspended. Butch had scarcely seemed to hear him. He had stood rubbing his head, saying, "Now I've heard everything!"

After dinner that night, the family assembled in the living room. Mother was going to read aloud. Since John's eyes had been strained by constant reading, he loved to sit and listen. His mother read beautifully and with such deep feeling that the characters seemed to come alive. But before she began, Margaret LaFarge wanted to discuss John's report card, which he had brought home that day. His marks, the report card stated, were excellent in all his subjects except penmanship. "Maybe John should take private writing lessons," his mother suggested.

The matter was discussed by the family. Some thought that it might be a good idea, but Bancel said, "John has a good mind, but a craftsman or mechanic he'll never be."

This judgment by his favorite brother made John wince. Bancel must have noticed, because he put in hurriedly, "I'll make a sailor of you yet. Next time Bill Smith and I go out, you can come along."

Bill Smith was one of Bancel's favorite friends. Imagine setting out to sea with both of them!

His mother, who was thinking her own thoughts, put in, "I've decided that John *should* have writing lessons. There's a man named Mr. Sisson on Spring Street who teaches penmanship. I'll have a talk with him." This settled, Mother asked what she should read.

"I have something I'd like to discuss first," John said. Thereupon all the grown-ups turned their attention toward the youngest son, as John recounted what had happened in school that day with Butch. "Wasn't it stupid for Butch to think all Catholics were Irish?" he asked. Besides, he went on, "Butch sounded as if there is something wrong with Catholics. Why?"

His mother explained that many people were prejudiced against those different from themselves. "Prejudice," she said, meant judging without good cause. Some were even so uncharitable as to wish harm to those they did not understand. Indeed, this caused most of the trouble in the world, she added.

"Are Catholics like that too?" John asked.

"Some are," his mother replied.

She then spoke of *Bonne Maman,* which was what the children called their Grandmother LaFarge. *Bonne Maman* had been just as unhappy about her son's marrying a Protestant as Nonna had been about her daughter's marrying a Catholic.

"But of course," their mother went on, "I was attracted to the Faith long before I ever became a Catholic."

While John was digesting this, his brother Oliver suddenly laughed aloud.

"What's so funny?" Emily asked.

Oliver explained that he has been thinking about the scene between Butch and John. "Maybe it would be better for John to have boxing lessons," he said.

That night John tossed in bed. Thoughts came so fast that he couldn't sleep. This business of some people's thinking themselves better than others was strange. Of course, it was natural to like some better than others. His favorite friends were still the Hills.

He was also very fond of red-headed Neil Fairchild, whose family were summer residents in Newport.

John remembered that he had fallen off the Fairchild's wharf one day when no one was around. It was sink or swim; so he swam—dog-paddled really—and he made the wharf. Bancel had been very proud of him.

Neil had encouraged him in another way. From the Fairchild's slowly drifting catboat, Neil did fancy dives. He was straight as a jackknife and scarcely made ripples on the water. Neil had insisted that John could dive just as well if he tried.

And John had done just that. Though he now admitted those first dives had been flat and far from perfect, he was no longer afraid to plunge. Times such as these spent with friends and reading books were what *he* considered "fun."

John's mother did arrange for him to take writing lessons from Mr. Sisson. So he went to the teacher's home on Spring Street after school. Mr. Sisson was a sad-faced young man who taught the Spencerian Method. This meant slanting script and making curlicues on the capital letters. This was supposed to be done with a strange, double-jointed pen. John tried and tried but, as lessons proceeded, Mr. Sisson's face grew sadder.

Finally, one late afternoon, when John had made what he considered a successful capital D, Mr. Sisson mournfully shook his head.

"I guess you just ain't made to write," he said. Then, without any ifs or buts, he told John not to come anymore.

The boy was crushed. He hated to go home and admit failure; so he decided to take a stroll. But instead of being comforting, this pilgrimage only seemed to make matters worse. Everywhere he was reminded that other members of their family had been successful. John wandered to the Old Stone Mill, a round structure made of neatly fitted slate. It had been built, as almost everyone believed, by an ancestor of his mother, the first Governor of Rhode Island (though some thought that Viking explorers had erected it). Nearby, in Touro Park, he gazed up at a statue of Uncle Matthew Calbraith Perry.

"If it hadn't been for him, East and West would have never met," Nonna had said about Uncle Matthew.

It hurt, having such distinguished ancestors and also a famous artist father, when he, his father's own namesake, could not even make a proper Spencerian D.

Gloomily he turned toward home.

When he confessed failure to his mother, she didn't

seem very upset. "Your Uncle Thomas Perry also has over-flexible fingers," she said. "As you know, he's Professor of English at Harvard and manages quite well."

Still, John's experience with Mr. Sisson left him quite shaken. He talked the matter over with Walter Hill, who was the proud possessor of a hand printing press. Maybe they could start a magazine, John suggested.

Both Walter and Perry thought this was a great idea. They would call their magazine *The Sunlight.* They would feature local news, information about Rhode Island history, and school items. *The Sunlight* would be sold for two cents a copy to friends and relatives. And John would be the editor.

John prepared the "copy" on a typewriter given to him by his Aunt Emily for Christmas. A set of woodcuts came with the printing press. These woodcuts had no relation to the type, nor for that matter did they seem to apply to anything else. Still, John decided, stories could be built around the woodcuts.

With that he let his imagination range. For each issue of *The Sunlight* he wrote an illustrated tale called "Trip to Mars." Since no one had ever been there, he figured, neither the stories nor the woodcuts could be contradicted.

Ten or twelve monthly issues of *The Sunlight* were

issued. He was an editor and a writer with a by-line. More. He was a printer, just like his grandfather—four times removed—Benjamin Franklin.

The background of John's boyhood was the sea. Beyond, by the cliffs, the sea was open and restless. Close by, in the harbor, the waters of Narragansett Bay were calm and placid. The voice of the sea told him and all Newport about the weather for tomorrow. As John lay in bed and listened, a roar from Easton's Beach would warn of stormy weather. After storms a distant bell would sound. This came from a buoy off Brenton's Reef, named after Jahleel Brenton, another ancestor of John's mother.

Almost as much as he loved the sea, John loved the sound of bells. In Newport, bells were melodious signals that told you what to do. At seven in the morning, the church bells rang for people to rise and start to work. At noon the lunch bell sounded. At one o'clock a bell was the signal to resume work. At nine in the evening the curfew rang. A new chime had recently joined the chorus. St. Mary's Church—the first Catholic Church in town—now sounded the Angelus bell at six in the morning and evening, as well as at twelve noon. This reminded the citizens not to forget their prayers.

During one of his frequent visits to the Redwood Library, John came upon a book telling how to install electric bells. Doubts about his mechanical ability were overcome in the hope that he, John LaFarge, could learn to make bells ring. His mother encouraged his interest. Before long, bells appeared in unlikely places all over the LaFarge house. And, wonder of wonders, they worked! A press of a button produced the sound of bells. Word of John's new-found talent spread, and he was soon installing bells all over the neighborhood.

Such were the sundry shapes and pieces of his boyhood. For the most part, the pattern of his life was even—more like the placid bay than the churning sea. John's delicate health, his lack of mechanical skill, and secret pangs about his absent father were as close to tragedy as he ever came.

Then one Sunday morning John awakened and hurriedly got dressed. This was the day Bancel had promised to take him out sailing with Bill Smith. He dashed downstairs, where Mother and most of the family were about to leave for Mass.

"Where's Bancel?" John asked.

"Still sleeping," his mother said. "He can make last Mass. You come along with us."

On the way to church, his brothers and sisters talked

about a gay party they had attended at the famous Newport Casino the night before.

Yawning, sister Emily said, "No wonder Bancel's sleepy, but I'm sure he'll wake in time."

John hoped his brother would. When they returned from church, though, Bancel was still asleep. Mother went upstairs to rouse him, and John followed. It was 11:30, and Bancel would have to hurry if he wanted to make last Mass.

"Why didn't you call me sooner?" he asked sleepily.

Just then, Bill Smith's voice sounded from downstairs.

"Are you ready, Bancel?" he called.

Bancel explained that he had overslept. Couldn't Bill wait for another hour, so that he could go to Mass? His friend said no, he thought their group had best get started. Although the day was fine, rain was predicted for later in the afternoon.

John thought his brother had forgotten the promise to take him on that sailing spree. He hadn't, though. Bancel said that he was sorry and that they would surely set out the following week.

To salve John's disappointment, Mother said she'd make pancakes for breakfast. While she was still stirring the batter, the skies clouded over and sounds from the sea announced a sudden squall.

John's sister Margaret, who was fond of Bill Smith, said, "I hope they didn't go too far out. Bill has a crippled friend along."

By the time Bancel came back from church the sun was shining again. Still, he was anxious. "A storm can be short and still be treacherous," he said.

He started to pace the floor, ignoring his mother's request to sit down and have some breakfast. "There's no sense looking in for trouble," she said.

Bancel, though, did not seem to hear. He must find out if his friends were safe. Bancel left the house.

John decided to watch at the window until his brother returned. Meanwhile, he would pray that all was well. The chimes on their grandfather's clock sounded many times before Bancel returned. When finally he flung himself into the house, his face was white and drawn. At first he could not even speak. Later, when words came, the family learned that Bill Smith's boat had capsized off Brenton's Reef. Bill had tried to save his crippled friend, but both were drowned.

Bancel covered his face and spoke through half-closed fingers. "If I had gone along, I might have helped," he said.

"It's possible," their mother replied, "but you might have been drowned, too."

"I don't know; I don't know," Bancel moaned.

He left then and went up to his room.

"How shocking," their mother said, "how shocking!"

And all the sisters cried, Margaret most of all.

John was tormented in a way he had never been before. He tried to pray and say "Thy will be done," but the words did not seem sincere. Why had God permitted Bill Smith to drown? Bill was doing his duty by trying to save a friend. If Bancel had been along he might have helped. Still, he had stayed behind to go to Mass. This was certainly a good reason. He gazed at the statue of the Child Jesus on the staircase post. He went upstairs, and from outside Bancel's door he heard his brother weeping.

"Dear God," John prayed, "don't let Bancel be so unhappy." Now, when he said "Thy will be done," the words did seem sincere. He went into his brother's room to comfort him.

When John was ten years old he and his mother again went to visit Nonna. Now she was living in the center of Philadelphia, with her daughter and son-in-law, Dr. and Mrs. William Pepper. The grown-ups seemed to love the city. There was a constant stream of visitors, both family and friends. During the periods when social activity slackened, Nonna's memory would again bring back the ghosts of Sergeants and Perrys and Benjamin Franklin. Departed commodores and statesmen sipped tea and ate crumpets with the living!

This stay was John's first experience in the city. He felt confined and lonely. He didn't care for houses built in blocks with no grounds and gardens around them. He yearned for the sound of the sea, and for air with a salty tang. Through Nonna's window, he watched the horse cars tinkling their way along Spruce Street, and thought of the chimes and bells of Newport. But what had been a dreary time for a homesick boy was climaxed by a most happy event—John's First Holy Communion. This took place in the Arch Street Convent of the Religious of the Sacred Heart. And he resolved that his soul should always remain, as far as possible, as white as the Host on his tongue—or the suit he wore on that occasion.

As he lay in bed that night thinking about all manner of things, John remembered the day when Bill Smith and his crippled friend had drowned—how he had tried to pray and the words seemed insincere. This, he saw now, had been to tempt his faith. Maybe such doubts would come again. But if so, he would pray to be strong.

3

Father Comes Home

IT WAS ONE MORNING during the winter of 1891, a few weeks after John's eleventh birthday. While he was having a lonely breakfast at the big dining room table, Emily, home from school, blew in from the cold. She had been out marketing and had stopped for the mail at the post office. John jumped up to help her carry the large bags of produce into the kitchen, where his mother was drying dishes.

"There's a letter here from Father," Emily announced. Then, she added softly "Most of the others look like bills."

"I don't know what I'd do without my small inheritance," Mrs. LaFarge said. She was so excited that she almost dropped the plate she was working on. She dried her hands on her apron, and her whole face took on a warm glow, as she almost snatched the letter from Emily. Then she sat down in the nearest chair. "Well now, let's see what your father has to say," she said.

44

As Mrs. LaFarge sat reading, Emily stacked groceries on the pantry shelves and arranged perishable foods in the ice box. When she had finished reading, their mother said, "Your father and Henry Adams are returning home to the United States. They both seemed to love the South Sea Islands."

To John, this news was no more than an echo from the past, when his father had returned from Japan with Henry Adams. He supposed it would be the same this time—his father would remain in New York. But his mother explained that their father was tired and expected to spend some time in Newport with the family. He wanted to rest a while before resuming his work on stained-glass windows, which was now his all-consuming interest.

Without meaning to judge, John heard his own voice say, "If Father wasn't tired, I guess he wouldn't bother to come home."

His mother's face was sad as she said, "I know how you must feel, John. But, as I've told you before, your father is a great artist and not like other people. He does not pretend to have behaved well toward the family. No matter what anyone might say about him, he is no hypocrite."

Although she seemed to take comfort from this thought, young John felt sure that his mother had suffered much because of her husband's absence. As for himself, he still would have preferred an ordinary, every-day father like Mr. Hill, and he decided not to mention that his father was expected to return—not even to Walter. One couldn't be sure he really would appear this time.

Soon after, an interesting couple came to spend a few days with the family. They were Frederick August Bartholdi—a famous sculptor—and his wife. Mrs. Bartholdi was the most beautiful woman John had ever seen. And she knew just how to get along with young people. So while her husband talked about his work, she and John roasted popcorn in the hearth.

The sculptor spoke chiefly of his masterpiece, the Statue of Liberty. The first design of this famous lady with a torch, he recalled, had been drafted in the studio of his good friend, John LaFarge, who was, he insisted, one of the greatest artists in the whole world.

Over the "pop-pop-pop," as hard kernels exploded into delicious puffs, came Monsieur Bartholdi's voice. He told how the first rivet had been placed in the Statue of Liberty on October 24, 1881. The following year, this giantess had loomed over the rooftops of Paris. On July 4, 1884, she was formally presented to the American Minister to France, Mr. L. P. Morton. Thereupon the statue had been dismantled for shipping.

"And now she stands in your harbor," the sculptor went on dramatically, "holding her torch in welcome to all."

It gave him great happiness, he added, to think that this master-piece was not only a symbol of freedom, but an everlasting bond of friendship between their countries.

Young John was deeply moved. He loved America—"her rocks and rills, her woods and templed hills"—and was proud to have Mr. Bartholdi in their house. His wife, who was still shaking the wire popper over hot coals, smiled at him. Popcorn, an American invention, was another bond between their countries.

John had put from his head Father's promise to return, but one day his mother told him he should not loiter after school. That very afternoon, she said, his father's ship would dock at Long Wharf, and they would go to meet him together.

"I'm sure your father is as anxious to see his name-sake as you are to see him," she added.

Although this was what John had always hoped for, down deep he now felt a little uneasy. In the first place, his father might not like him. Even more, John was not certain about the way *he* was going to feel. Still, the idea of being able to produce a father of his own had its points, and John found himself telling

friends and teachers alike that he had to hurry home.
No, he could not join Walter nor stop by at the Redwood Library for a book. His father was returning
from the South Seas. Now, anyone who had wondered
would know that he really had a father!

That afternoon John and his mother drove in a cab
to Long Wharf. While they were waiting on the pier,
the boy wondered if his father would have the celebrated Mr. Adams with him. Questions buzzed in his
head like bees. He was excited but anxious too. The
ship had already anchored and people were moving
down the gangplank. Which one was his father?—
which?

After a while, a most unlikely father—quite old-
looking and tanned and bearded—bounded toward
them. Surely, this could not be the one, John thought.
But then, why should a strange man hug and kiss my
mother? The big man turned then, looked down and
said, "So this is my namesake."

Young John didn't know whether to extend his hand
to be shaken. His hesitation was short-lived, because
Father gave him a friendly whack on the shoulder,
rumpled his hair, and said, "I hear you're quite a prod-
igy. We'll have to get acquainted."

This was what John also wanted, to get acquainted.
Shyly, he said, "It's good to see you, Father."

The big man looked down and said,
"So this is my namesake."

He was about to say more, but his father had turned away. He must see to his luggage and attend to this and that. The bearded man who was his father darted here and there, talking to customs officers and saying farewell to fellow passengers.

John gazed up at his mother. He noticed that her shining eyes were following every motion, every gesture of her husband. The boy could remember having seen that special smile on his mother's lips, that shine in her eye, before. It was the way she looked when she read that letter. It was the way Mrs. Hill smiled, too, when her husband had come home that day.

With a sense that perhaps all was well in the world, John said, "I think I'm going to like Father. He's interesting."

And interesting the artist was. After his return there was never a dull moment in the house. The air seemed charged with electricity. When Father engaged in a discussion, his thoughts came fast, his words flowed like a restless rushing stream. When he spoke of far-off places, the whole world of sights and sounds and people moved into the Newport living room.

There were other times, though, when father's presence created a wintry gloom. Everyone had to walk on tiptoe then, and converse in whispers. His thoughts could not be broken by the sound of children's voices; he could not be concerned with household chores. A slamming door or the sound of laughter would put him into a rage. He shouted; he scolded; he paced the floor. At first these shifting moods frightened John a little, but his brothers and sisters scarcely seemed to notice them.

It was just their father's "artistic temperament," their mother would explain. Father didn't want to hurt anyone. She knew that he felt sorry when he did.

This seemed to be so, because, sometimes after an outburst of temper, Father would apologize and blame his behavior on the fact that he was "a sick man." John couldn't help wondering why—if his father's health was so poor—he had strength enough to travel all over the world. He could not understand that his father was creating some very beautiful design in his mind. This was so difficult that it sometimes made an artist ill, although he was physically very healthy.

Often, quite suddenly, the artist had to depart for New York in order to contact patrons and supervise the manufacture of the new kind of stained-glass he had invented. Without his direction, the pieces might not be properly put together, or his artistic concept might be misunderstood. In his studio on Tenth Street, he could labor undisturbed.

While in New York the artist spent much time with his mother, *Bonne Maman*. Returning to Newport, he spoke of many LaFarge relatives. One day, during Christmas vacation, John's father suddenly decided to take his youngest son along to visit *Bonne Maman*. "It's high time you got to know my side of the family better," he said.

On the train Father was entertaining and attentive and full of questions. He asked John about his schooling, his pastimes, and his aims. What did his son wish to be when he grew up?

John found himself confiding in his father—how he had difficulty with manual skills, that he had not done very well in art class. No matter how he tried, the boy said, the pictures he saw in his mind did not come out that way on paper. "Should I keep trying?" John asked his father.

"No, John," his father replied. "I don't believe talent can be learned. True, there are those who call themselves artists, but they are actually no more than craftsmen. Such men are hypocrites."

He then encouraged John to speak of the things he enjoyed most. Man did best at work he loved, Father said.

Books **and reading** were closest to his heart, John confided. **He loved** words, and could even make his way in some **strange** foreign languages, such as Danish or Icelandic. He was also deeply affected by music and was taking piano lessons. He was doing quite well at this, his music teacher had told him, in spite of fingers with a tendency to fly in all directions.

"What kind of music do you like the best, Father?" John asked.

Here, the artist laughed so loud that people in the train turned around to look.

"If you want the truth, son," his father said, "I like best the music that makes least sound."

His father admitted that he had absolutely no ear for music. "So you see, we're even," he said. "You are no artist and I am no musician."

John was proud to be put on the same plane. Besides, his father seemed to approve of his love for learning.

"You'll find out in good time what you want to be," he said.

The stay at *Bonne Maman's* reminded John of the times he had visited Nonna. Grandmother LaFarge also talked a great deal about her family. Besides his living relatives, John was also introduced to shadowy ancestors from the past. "You favor our side of the family," *Bonne Maman* told her grandson.

The boy smiled, because Nonna had said exactly the same thing. But he did not mention this.

The talk went on, just as it had at Nonna's. But

instead of commodores and statesmen, *Bonne Maman* boasted about scholars and painters and royal families. Her patriotism stemmed from the soil of France.

"If it were not for the Marquis de Lafayette," she said, "America would still be a colony of Britain."

John thought how shocked Nonna would be by such a statement.

LaFarges of all ages came to call. They talked about important members of the family, and, as John sat sipping rich hot chocolate with whipped cream, he wondered again why people had to consider themselves better.

John was in his second year of high school.

The house was no longer full of family. His brothers were away at college, and the girls often visited their friends in other cities. All the girls had many suitors, but Emily would probably be the first to marry.

John had continued to be a superior student. He was widely read on almost any subject, and was respected by his teachers. He had a real gift for languages, and could speak French fluently. He often stopped at the Redwood Library to take out books. Since his boyhood days a wing had been added to the building. Before, this area had been a large back porch, which people rarely visited. But for him this quiet spot had been a magical hiding place, where he had spent long summer afternoons reading sea stories and biographies.

One day on the way home from school, he was hailed by Walter Hill. "Let's go fishing before it gets too dark," Walter said as he caught up with John. "What say?"

"Can't," John replied. "Have to catch up on some studying."

"You're such a grind," was Walter's wry comment.

They had remained best friends, but John often knew that Walter thought he was too serious. Many of his companions did. John had heard himself described as the "absent-minded professor." He admitted there was some truth in this. With his head in the clouds, he was forgetful of small things, and his mind had a way of wandering.

Nearing his home, John saw his shadow cast on the pavement. Tall, thin, and loose-jointed, he had a shock of hair that refused to stay put. Maybe he looked like an "absent-minded professor," too. . . . He now smoothed the strands back with his free hand.

As he went inside, his sister Margaret announced that their father was home and in a dreadful mood.

"Better walk on tiptoe," she cautioned.

John had grown accustomed to his father's habits, and was no longer surprised at his sudden appearances. This time, however, John was somewhat annoyed. It was very well for his father to come and go, he thought, but it did seem unfair for him to upset the entire household. He put down his books and went into the kitchen for a glass of milk. Mother still insisted on this between-meal habit. She and his sisters still babied him, and John sometimes wished they'd stop mentioning his "delicate health."

Mother seemed to be preparing a most elaborate meal.

"Why all the fuss?" John asked.

She explained that Henry Adams was expected —and she hoped that his visit would put her husband in a better mood.

John hoped so too, but at the moment there were other things on his mind. He was taking a French test the following day and wanted to study.

"You'd better go up to your own room, then, and close the door," his mother suggested.

For some reason, though, John found it hard to concentrate. This happened far too frequently. Now he asked himself why. He imagined that one of the reasons was that he really hadn't been feeling very well.

Then, too, he was often worried because he seemed

unable to decide on a future career. He continually read biographies in order to find out how other men had made up their minds about what they wished to be. John often asked himself and his family about it, but no answer had as yet come. Still, he felt certain that the choice would be made when it was time. Now, though, he must get back to work.

He was so deep in study that he was startled when his sister Frances knocked on the door.

"Dinner's ready," she called.

John left his books. He was suddenly curious to meet his father's legendary traveling companion, Henry Adams. John knew, of course, of the great man's background, and his famous ancestors, Presidents John and John Quincy Adams. More personal information had been relayed by John's sisters, who blithely called their distinguished guest "Uncle Henry." From their point of view he was "positively charming," and had an air of romantic sadness.

This, his mother had explained, was because Mr. Adams' wife had died when she was very young, and he had never recovered from that loss.

John had to admit that Mr. Adams was indeed delightful. His speech and manner marked him as a true aristocrat. He was attentive to everyone, but especially to their mother. It was regrettable, he said, that more women were not like her. Too many were trying to do man's work in the world. "The natural role of woman is wife and mother," Mr. Adams said.

His face became sad then, and John supposed Mr. Adams was thinking about his wife. Emily must have had the same idea, for she started to chat of trivial matters, as if trying to divert him. Soon he was downing a hearty meal.

"This is the best food I've ever eaten outside of France," he said, and their mother flushed with pleasure at the compliment.

When dinner was over, they all went into the living room. Father was in high humor now. He brought out large folios of drawings he had done on an island in the South Seas. As he handed them around, the artist spoke of the charming natives there.

"Look!" he said, "those simple people have the bearing of Egyptian royalty. They have grace and color and dignity."

Mr. Adams agreed. Then the artist went on to say that he hated the pharisaical habit of finding fault with people because they were different.

"We are all children of the common Father," he concluded.

And John felt a surge of warm affection for his father then. What he had expressed was also John's view. Men should be bound together in brotherhood, regardless of differences. Wasn't this what the Bible taught?

Now, it came to John that he might want to be a priest. The thought had occurred to him before. It was strange that his father's words had revived this dream. Perhaps, though, this would also prove a passing fancy.

At that point the two men began to discuss Mr. LaFarge's latest experiments with stained-glass. With that the family was forgotten, and they spoke excitedly about seeing France again.

"We must spend more time in Chartres Cathedral and Mont-St.-Michel," Mr. Adams said. "Someday I'm going to write a book about those historic windows in stained-glass."

"I'm sure you will," the artist replied. "And I still have much to learn from them."

As they continued their talk—unaware of anything except the subject—John suddenly understood the chief difference between his father and men like Mr. Hill. To his father, art came first. His feelings about his family were weakened by a greater love. John felt quite certain Mother must have suffered.

One day soon after he discovered this was so. John and his mother were taking a walk along Easton's

Beach. The skies were bleak and gray, the water sullen and the color of unpolished silver.

"There's something I want you to know," his mother blurted out. "Your father has never properly looked after us. He means well, but many times he forgets his family duties."

After saying this much, Mother dipped back into her memories. She spoke about her girlhood in Newport, how she had been courted by many suitors. One of these had been the famous author, Henry James. Some people thought that he had written about her in his book *Portrait of a Lady*. She went on to tell how Henry James and his brother William had wanted to be painters. Her husband, though, had discouraged them from careers in art; he thought that their talents took other forms.

"Your father gave them wise advice," Margaret La-Farge went on. "They have both done brilliantly in other fields."

John, who was curious about the author who had put his mother in a book, asked, "What happened to Mr. Henry James?"

"He renounced his American citizenship," his mother said, "and now he's living in England." Her son romantically supposed that this exile had been prompted by a broken heart.

"And William James teaches psychology at Harvard and writes wonderful books on the subject," his mother went on. "Maybe someday you'll go to college there."

For John, though, any idea of college lay in the distant future. During his second year at Rogers High School, his education was interrupted. He became ill with severe stomach pains which doctors could not diagnose. He could not eat even his favorite foods. Most of the time he had to remain in bed. When he became so listless that he didn't even want to read, his mother decided to move the family to New York. There she could consult with specialists and have her husband share the responsibility of their son's illness.

"It's about time I put my foot down," she declared. "At least for a time our family will be living under the same roof."

4

At Harvard

THE LAFARGE FAMILY moved back to Newport after two years' stay in the city. On their first Sunday morning home, John stopped by at the Hill's after Mass. Walter suggested they celebrate their reunion by taking one of the small boats out off Easton's Point. They could do a bit of fishing, and, after that, John could come back for dinner.

This invitation had been echoed by all the Hills, who seemed happy to have him back. Catherine—a lovely young lady now—had put aside her finishing-school manners and roundly hugged him.

John smiled to himself, remembering that for some reason he hadn't felt shy with Catherine. She seemed almost like a sister.

He had just stopped by to see them, John had told the Hills, but he could not stay. Maybe they would give him a "rain check."

Any time, the whole family chorused. But Walter

could not wait to hear about John's impressions of New York. "What did you enjoy most?" he asked.

"My ride home from the hospital in an electric hansom," John humorously replied.

"Oh come now, be serious."

There had been many exciting experiences—concerts, operas, museums, but most of all, interesting new friends. "Soon I'll tell you all about it," he had said. "You won't be able to shut me up." Now though, he had to be off; he had a problem to solve.

Now that he was home, John yearned for an old-time family conference. But this was impossible. Most of his brothers and sisters were no longer there.

Both Grant and Emily had married, and Grant was living in New York, a partner in the firm of Heins and LaFarge, Architects.

And Emily—whom he missed more than all others—was a young matron, residing in the suburbs of Philadelphia.

Bancel was also away somewhere with canvas and easel, painting. During his first year as a medical student, he had developed a serious infection in one eye. His sight was impaired and he had decided against becoming a doctor. Instead, he had taken up painting, and proven himself a gifted artist. He now also handled the family financial affairs, and with great ability.

Nor could he count on the others, John thought. Oliver and the girls were in such demand for weekends away at parties that their mother had nicknamed them "the boarders." As far as his father was concerned, he had resumed his old routine and remained mostly in New York. Thus, the only one around to give advice was his mother, and John suspected that she would again say, "You must make up your own mind."

Everything had seemed to be settled. After his appendicitis operation (for that was how the doctor finally diagnosed his illness), John had not been able to attend school regularly. With the aid of a tutor, though, he had kept up with studies and passed the entrance examinations for Columbia University. Oliver had been pleased, since this was his alma mater. But Bancel had not. He felt that John would be happier at Harvard. This difference of opinion had created doubts in John's mind.

At lunch John brought up the subject again, reminding his mother that there was little time left. If he did decide to go to Harvard, he would have to take entrance examinations there. "And even if I pass, it might be too late," he said.

"Don't worry, John," his mother said. "Of course you'll pass. And if you lived in Cambridge," she added, "Uncle Thomas and Aunt Lilla could look after you."

Frances, who had just arrived, put in scoffingly, "Oh, sure, everyone will make sure that John drinks his milk."

"Enough out of you!" he shouted, pretending to be angry.

To his mother John said that Uncle Thomas probably had more important things to do than coddle stray nephews. Besides, he didn't want to go on being treated like a child.

This had not been her intention, his mother said. "If you are still doubtful," she added, "Why don't you take a trip to Saunderstown and consult your brother Grant?"

John wasn't sure he should. Grant had been quite ill and it didn't seem fair to bother him. Still, he needed advice badly. And Grant could give it to him.

On the train John blamed himself for much of the indecision. Although he was still interested in the priesthood, there were certain aspects of this life that made him hesitate. The average parish priest, like Father Cronan, had so little time to read and study. Many of their duties required strenuous activity.

Then, too, John remembered his past daydreams. Once he had wanted to be a winder of clocks, and in fancy scampered up spiral stairs to church steeples. As a commodore, he had sailed unchartered seas to lands yet undiscovered. His idea of the priesthood might also be subject to change. He was confused; he hoped that Grant could help him.

But when he reached his brother's summer cottage, the front door was opened by a man John had never seen before. The stranger put a finger to his lips to signify the need for silence. After leading the young man into a small den on tiptoe, he closed the door. Even then he still spoke in hushed tones. "You must be John," he said.

John nodded.

"Let me introduce myself," he said. "I'm Theodore Roosevelt. My wife and Grant's have gone shopping; so I'm holding down the fort."

Grant had often spoken of his friendship with Mr. Roosevelt. The two had gone on hunting trips together out West and had also explored the Rocky Mountain territory. They also had a mutual interest in the conservation of wild life.

John was drawn to the man immediately. Even in whispered conversation he showed his vitality and warmth. He also proved to be a good listener, and John found himself asking advice about his conflicts.

He half-expected Mr. Roosevelt to be critical. Instead he was most assuring, and pointed out that there was actually no reason for John to decide about the future then and there. Time would clarify his doubts.

As for colleges, Mr. Roosevelt felt that a young man of his interests would find the climate at Harvard more congenial.

John was grateful for this advice, so freely and generously given. He decided to take entrance examinations for Harvard. There was no need even to bother Grant.

When his brother awakened, they had a brief visit together. Both spoke of their admiration for Mr. Roosevelt. Grant predicted that "T. R.," as many called him, would not remain Police Commissioner of New York for long. He was a leader of men and excellent presidential timber, Grant thought.

John journeyed to Cambridge, Massachusetts, with a sprinkling of undergraduates. Neil Fairchild was the only one he knew. They sat together on the train.

At first they chatted about the past, and John spoke warmly of his long friendship with all the Fairchild family. He recalled that his first dive had been taken from off their catboat. "That wasn't much of a performance," he said.

Neil laughed and said, "Anyhow, you made it."

They talked about treks to The Point, where nautical-minded Newport old-settlers had always welcomed the small boys. There had been a character

called "Skipper Hank." Neil admitted that this salty old fellow used to terrify him, with gory tales of scaly-headed monsters of the sea. "Whenever we climbed the cliffs I expected to see one," he said with a smile.

After a while, Neil shifted their talk to the present. He wanted to do well at Harvard, he confided to his friend. But he was also resolved to lead a well-balanced life. He meant to study as much as would be required to "get by," as he called it, and also to try out for sports; but he was not going to neglect the girls at

John was drawn to Theodore Roosevelt immediately, and was soon asking his advice.

Radcliffe College nearby. His advice to John was that he should do the same.

"You've become terribly serious," he said.

John admitted that maybe he was too bookish. But this didn't mean that he wasn't fond of people. Indeed, he insisted, he was deeply drawn to the human race, in a general way.

"That sounds like a cover-up for shyness," Neil said.

"After we're settled, let's get together with some dates."

Those first days in Cambridge before classes began were dismal ones for John. He was lodged in a brownstone house of ancient vintage. His landlady who spoke of herself as a "genteel spinster," was loud-voiced and untidy. She reminded John of a character out of Dickens. Furthermore, she had never learned to cook. The only other boarder was a glum, sallow-faced student from Upstate New York, whose only pleasure seemed to be ranting about "this awful world."

In contrast to Newport, this home-away-from-home was very bleak, indeed. John sometimes wondered what his mother would have said about his sketchy meals. Often he cooked his own breakfast, and for lunch snatched a sandwich at the Hasty Pudding Club. His landlady's dinners were so tasteless that John sometimes pretended to have eaten at a restaurant.

Later, when he was invited to join relatives or a teacher for meals, his menus improved. He was always welcome at the home of his cousin Miss Agnes Irwin, who was Dean of Radcliffe College. Her specialty was a soup which, to the hungry student, tasted like the nectar of the gods.

John knew that it would be folly to neglect his health. After classes began he resolved to combine study with routine exercise. He started to go to the gym, do a bit of rowing on the Charles River, and sometimes took long bicycle rides under the moonlit sky. Evidently this activity was too much. Instead of growing healthier, he had spells of weakness and decided to slow down.

In his freshman year there were required subjects. One of these was English. At first John was somewhat annoyed at being forced to register for courses that he did not choose himself. Later, though, this seemed a lucky break. Otherwise he might not have met Professor Charles Copeland—better known to the students as "Copey." His classes were like the tangy breezes wafted from Narragansett Bay. Copey encouraged students to express themselves freely. They must write what they believed and not hold back, he told them. They should not be afraid of offending.

His classes were always jammed full of eager listeners, and Copey's "readings" reminded John of those evenings in Newport when his mother had read aloud. In striving for perfection, John had been slow to submit his literary efforts. Finally, though, after much labor and rewriting, he did hand in an essay.

After selecting this from a pile of papers, Copey

squinted and said, "LaFarge, your handwriting is Gothic. That's the best I can say for it."

In spite of this comment, Professor Copeland had praise for what John had written. LaFarge's essay had fine form, he said, and substance, and reflected a rich background of reading. This approval prompted John to write another essay, this one dealing with days long past, when he had gone for writing lessons to Mr. Sisson's. Amusingly he told of his tragic failure to make a Spencerian D.

Later, when Copey selected this paper to read aloud, peals of laughter sounded throughout the class. Many students who had always seemed somewhat in awe of John now approached him. It was rare that a scholar should also have such a keen sense of humor, they told him.

If these English classes were lively and informal, John could not say the same about the spirit of Harvard in general. For the most part, John had the feeling that friendliness was considered in bad taste. He was often amused by the clannishness of certain groups. His own friendships were formed strictly on the basis of mutual interests.

It had sometimes been suggested that because of his impressive ancestry John really belonged in the exclusive campus social set, which preferred not to mix socially with anyone who had arrived much later than the Mayflower.

In spite of his family connections, John soon realized that he did not quite belong. He did not care, but it puzzled him, until he gradually came to understand the reason. More than once he had noticed a change of attitude in some classmate after learning that John was a Catholic. They were amazed; he *couldn't* be.

Actually, he was the one to be amazed about the strange ideas many students had of the Catholic Church. Obviously these false notions had been taught in the home, and again he was saddened by people's need to consider themselves better than others, instead of trying to achieve brotherhood.

On the whole, John enjoyed his courses. Most of the faculty were learned men. Still, it sometimes seemed that certain subjects were presented in a vacuum. At Harvard no religion was taught, except in the Divinity School. It was popular just then to downgrade all values that could not be proved by pure reason. Therefore, to speak of religion was unfashionable. This seemed unfair to John, who liked to examine all points of view.

This caused him trouble during a psychology course given by no less than Mr. William James. Because he was the older brother of the author, Henry—who had been in love with Mother—John was deeply interested in what he would have to say. So he listened hard, but for him Mr. James' teaching of psychology seemed woefully unbalanced. It was as though the human mind was no more than some flabby mass stuffed into a skull.

Troubled by this view, John asked, "But what about God and man's mystical experience, Mr. James?"

He was sharply told that such speculation did not concern men of reason.

John did not agree, but let this pass.

Sometimes John humorously reflected that he was a failure at "fitting in." He occasionally joined Neil and a few friends for a party, but these gatherings always ended up the same way. John didn't drink liquor or dance and had no wish to "paint the town red." So, when he was present, the group sat around and talked. Although Neil insisted that everyone had thought he was charming, John was sure the party would have been more lively if he had remained at home.

Occasionally, too, John even felt set apart from members of his own faith. He wondered if this might be because he hadn't attended parochial school. Most of his Catholic friends who had, didn't seem to mind that their Church in Cambridge was so unattractive.

Saint Paul's was a plain wooden structure, ugly outside and equally dreary within. The religious services were uninspiring. The pastor spoke mainly of the state of his own health, or threatened hell-fire for his parishioners.

If the Catholic Faith was to be judged by the performance there, John thought, what a false impression Protestants must have. And what a contrast to the big Protestant church on Copley Square. It amused John that this church owed much of its beauty to the masterful paintings and stained-glass windows by a Catholic artist named John LaFarge.

John's strongest influence was his desire for learning, and during those years at Harvard his scholarship won the respect of both students and professors. As a symbol of his labors, a coveted Phi Beta Kappa key (for fine scholastic achievement) dangled from his watch-chain.

As for lighter moments, none were so enjoyable as the time he spent at the home of his uncle, Thomas Sergeant Perry. There John joined a musical trio, in which he played the piano part. His aunt and uncle were both extremely gifted people. Not only was his uncle a professor at Harvard, he was also a famous literary critic. Aunt Lilla was both a poet and a painter of some renown. For John, though, these talents were secondary to the warmth and generosity of their home life.

During John's junior year, brother Bancel became engaged to Miss Mabel Hooper of Boston. She was one of five lovely sisters, and John learned that the sixth one had been the wife still mourned by Uncle Henry Adams. John was overjoyed that Bancel had found happiness.

It had been Bancel's egg collection that first caused John to marvel about creation; it had been Bancel's financial help that made it possible for his youngest brother to go to college. And now he would again have to rely on Bancel's help.

It had become crystal clear that for John there was no other life than that of a priest. He had been advised to pursue this vocation at the University of Innsbruck in Austria. To do so would be very costly; and besides, he was not sure how the family would feel about his becoming a priest.

As always, Bancel came to the rescue by promising to share expenses. But even this did not insure John's future. Both Grant and his father expressed doubts about his decision. To them it seemed impulsive, if not rash.

John could understand why they felt that way. Nonetheless, he knew—and deep down had always known—that his life must be spent in the service of God.

Because Grant wished to be fair and objective, he had invited his friend Theodore Roosevelt to take part in the family conference. The Commissioner sat and listened as they spoke. When each one had finished voicing his doubts and objections, Mr. Roosevelt said: "I have listened, and since you asked me to join you, I will speak plainly. This boy has a vocation. God has sent him certain lights and certain graces. It would be folly not to let him follow them."

"That's how I feel, too," John's mother said.

John knew how difficult this must have been for her. This was a special kind of leave-taking. Thus, when they parted at the station, he was not surprised to see—for the first time in his life—his mother weep.

5

Fateful Decision

JOHN'S LODGINGS in Innsbruck were on the second floor at Number 3 Adamgasse. The house and street were separated by a cold mountain stream that rushed through the town. In the same building was a coffee factory, with a water-wheel that operated machinery day and night. He could have lived in the Residence maintained by the Jesuit faculty, but because of the many rules he had decided to rent a room in a private home.

John had never been so lonely in his life as he was during those early days at Innsbruck. The Alpine air was bracing and the scenery beautiful, but the majestic mountains seemed only to increase his loneliness. He started to have a recurrent dream, in which the water-wheel became a ship's engine carrying him back to America.

To take his thoughts away from home, John rented a piano and spent much time practising. Soon, though, he began to realize that there was little sense in staying alone so much. What he needed was to get out and make friends. John decided to start with students at Frau Evers', where he took his meals. Three other seminarians also enjoyed Frau Evers' delicious fare. Till now John had remained somewhat aloof from them. This must be changed, he decided.

At dinner that evening he broke into his best German, which was not very good. In turn, the students tried out their English, which John decided was scarcely better. From then on, meals were enlivened by an exchange of views, which sometimes led to arguments.

One of the German students enjoyed scoffing at America and democracy. He claimed that the idea of "equality for all" was stupid. Those fit to rule should rule, he maintained, and the others should follow.

John always asked what made men "fit."

Boldness and clarity of thought, he was told.

Heinrich Chardon, a Rhinelander, usually remained silent during these debates. If he did happen to join in, it was in the role of peacemaker. He and John became close friends. When the others weren't present they had many interesting talks. Heinrich often mentioned the deep ancient rivalry existing among many of the European countries. If these bad feelings were not

curbed, he feared they would surely cause a war someday.

One evening the two friends went to the Town Hall
to attend a political rally. Most of the audience were
peasants and working men. The speakers at the rally
were both clergymen and lay people about equally
divided. The clergy spoke about the moral necessity of
the betterment of man. True followers of Christ, they
said, must be concerned with the plight of the poor
and downtrodden. In the crowd a Socialist shouted,
"Religion has failed the people! Instead of depending
on prayer, we must unite and demand justice!"

Although John could not agree, he knew that these
social problems must be solved. In America, even a
simple, unknown man could achieve success, through
the democratic process. But here in Europe there was
little opportunity for improvement. Thus, the poor had
to be content with their poverty, and peasants toiled
almost like slaves. All around he could see desperate
people turning to the materialism of Karl Marx.

About the political situation John wrote to his
mother: "I will need a strong will and a calm mind to
discover the truth."

John's studies at Innsbruck were directed toward
the quest of truth. Unlike at Harvard, the students

were in close touch with their professors, both in and out of class. All courses except Church History were conducted in Latin. John's gift for languages now served him well. He could read many ancient manuscripts in the original form.

For the good of his soul and to make new friends, John joined the Sodality of the Blessed Virgin Mary. His musical talent was soon discovered, and he was appointed organist for their weekly meetings. He played hymns on the small harmonium in the frescoed Princes' Chapel of the Jesuit University church.

Before long he discovered a group of his own countrymen. This colony called itself, "The American Exiles." Together, they reminisced about the United States and felt a little less alien. From letters they received they shared the latest news of events in America. One startling bit of information, however, came in another way. Late one night along the Adamgasse, the sound of the water-wheel was drowned out by a voice.

"Extra . . . extra!" a newsboy cried. This was followed by another, "President McKinley murdered!"

For a while the American students spoke of nothing else but the President's assassination. Later, their interest turned to the new President, Theodore Roosevelt. John was not surprised that Grant's friend had become President.

"I mightn't be here if it hadn't been for him," John told his fellow Americans.

It had not been his intention to boast, but they all seemed impressed that one of their group should be on speaking terms with the new President. They pelted John with questions. What was Mr. Roosevelt like? How did John happen to know him?

"The President is actually my brother's friend," he explained. "I've only met him a few times." Nonetheless, John was elected to give a speech about the President, which took place on Thanksgiving Day, when his fellow countrymen came together for a turkey dinner.

As Christmas approached, John's loneliness again returned. Long walks through half-medieval Innsbruck at dusk did not raise his spirits; when he tried to read, his thoughts turned instead to home. He decided to go to Munich for the holidays. There he visited museums, went to the theater, and attended Midnight Mass.

After returning to Innsbruck, John moved into the Jesuit Residence. There, for the first time, he was content. In this community of men whose lives were devoted to God he no longer felt lonely. Separation from the family seemed a small sacrifice now.

Soon after moving into the Residence, he made his

first spiritual retreat. During that period of silence and meditation, he felt he was actually in touch with the living Christ. For the first time John had a sense of what his own inner life could mean.

John was often amazed that his health held up so well. Life in the Jesuit Residence was rugged. The benches were hard; the food was simple; there was little heat in any of the buildings except the bedrooms. Often, students went to classes swathed in coats and galoshes as if for an old-fashioned sleigh ride, and, in the chapel, the holy water sometimes froze solid in the bronze fonts.

Then one day John was reminded that there were other seasons besides winter. He received a letter from his mother, telling him that in the spring she and his sister Margaret were going to tour the Continent. Since John had no vacation plans, couldn't he join them in England? Their first stop would be Rye Sussex, at the Mermaid Inn. They had chosen this place because Mr. Henry James lived in the vicinity. When he had learned about their proposed visit, the author had suggested renewing an old and precious friendship.

"I think you would also enjoy meeting Mr. James, John," his mother said at the close of the letter.

*Often the students went to class swathed
in coats and galoshes.*

This might be so, John thought, but at the moment he was more interested in the rest of the news. His mother, who for so long had been one to stay at home, was to be a traveler. He wanted to help her to enjoy this trip abroad.

On the appointed day John met his mother and sister at the Mermaid Inn. After the first greetings were over, Mother admitted she could find no fault with the way her son looked.

"You've actually filled out," she said. "The food at Innsbruck must be good." This surprised her, because she had been told that Jesuits ate quite sparingly. She also hoped John had been sensible about the cold and bundled up.

"Absolutely," her son said. "Sometimes I even wear galoshes to class."

"That's just one of your little jokes," she said.

John had never seen his mother so carefree. She chatted merrily on about the Inn. Except for the food—which was a bit too doughy for American tastes—the place was enchanting. "Especially my own room," she said. "It reminds me of Noah's Ark."

Soon after they were settled, Mr. James was announced. John was interested in this great novelist, who was criticized by many of his countrymen for having become a British subject. He also was reputed to be a snob, but for his old friend "Margaret Perry" he had the warmest greetings.

Mr. James let it be known that he intended to play host to the visitors. He would show them the countryside and not permit them to suffer the poor food at the inn. Most of their meals would be at his home. This stately residence, called Lamb House, was staffed by servants who catered to the appetites of his foreign friends.

During long hikes over the lush Sussex Meadows, Henry James and Mrs. LaFarge spoke mostly of the past. John and Margaret did not join in these conversations. They seemed private and belonged to a period unrelated to themselves. More than once, though, the author expressed admiration for their father, and one evening, during a delectable meal at Lamb House, he addressed them all on this subject.

"The wisdom of John LaFarge changed my entire life," he said. "While watching me dabble in paints, he encouraged me to write. Not only is he one of the greatest artists in America, he also has a gift for steering people where they belong."

Their mother flushed with pleasure at this praise. "Yes," she agreed, "my husband does have a gift for guiding people."

Mr. James then questioned John about his career. He could understand anyone's wanting to get away from crass competition of the modern world. Did John expect to enter the Jesuits?

"No!" his mother exclaimed, before John could speak. "You wouldn't dream of such a thing, would you, John?"

Though the idea had never crossed his mind until then, John was too tongue-tied to say "No."

During their two weeks of daily contact, Mr. James sometimes seemed moody. John hoped they had not stayed too long. He had learned about artistic "temperament" from his father. Soon after the family arrived in London, John received a gracious letter from Mr. James and his doubts dissolved.

My Dear John [*it read*]:

I rejoiced to hear from you, all the more that your news seems to be the best. I am particularly glad that your mother's London quarters soothe and satisfy her from the first. You have all clearly the gift of falling on your feet. If the world were more solicitously arranged, I should now be in London, too, to give you my long experience of it—an idea that makes me wishful as I think of a hundred places to which I might personally conduct you. . . .

Little limited Rye has since you left kept up its simple habit of breaking into grassy walks and mak-

*ing small unlifted pictures of flushing with pink
sunsets. . . .*

*So I bid you all goodnight, or good morning, while
I listen in the intense stillness of the Rye small hours
to the scratching of my pen, the ticking of my old
clock and, (I am sorry to say) to the patter of rain
in my garden.*

*Give my best to your companions, and believe
in the great pleasure our reunion here has
brought. . . .*

> *Affectionately,*
> *Henry James*

All in all, that English vacation was one of the most
enjoyable John had ever known. Even more than his
own enjoyment, his mother's delight in every moment
had given him deep pleasure. When she and Margaret
boarded the ship for home, though, her merriment was
gone.

"When will we see you again, John?" she asked tear-
fully.

He countered with a bit of teasing.

"Never, if you don't stop dampening my shirt front
with your tears," John said. "Remember, I have to iron
my own clothes."

Three years had passed since then, and John had
recently returned to Innsbruck from a vacation in

Newport. He sat in his bare, uncluttered room. A few of his friends were going to the inn at Schwartz for an evening of festivity. There, over mugs of beer and savory food, they would relax and engage in small talk. This was a good way to unwind after too much study.

Heinrich Chardon knocked on the door and said, "We're about ready to leave. Are you ready, John?"

"I'm not going," John said, as he opened the door to his friend.

Heinrich was not one to pry. After he was assured that his friend was not ill, he ducked out and called back over one shoulder, "Enjoy your solitude."

John seriously doubted that he would. He wanted to stay because he was troubled. He would be ordained to the priesthood in less than two months. Why, then he asked himself, was he not happier? He had no doubts about a calling to serve God, and yet it seemed he had come so far but not far enough.

Before returning from the United States, he had visited many parish priests, and each time he had asked himself, Is this what I truly want?

"Not quite," the answer came, "Not quite."

In the silence John seemed again to see the small iron stove in the Newport nursery. He heard his voice ask, "What do I want to be when I grow up?"

But he was near his goal now, and the answer was still "not quite." Why? John asked the bare walls of his room. But thinking no longer helped, and so he prayed.

Then suddenly, it was clear. Those visits to the parish priests had bothered him because he did not fit into the parish picture. His concept of the priestly life for himself was the Jesuit life. He wanted to live under the rules of poverty and obedience, in a company of men walking humbly in the footsteps of Christ. There was no other way for him.

John applied for membership in the Society of Jesus and was accepted. It was decided, with the permission of his bishop, that he should be ordained before entering the Society. On July 26, 1905, he was ordained along with his class. His first Mass was attended by his mother, sister Margaret, and other relatives and friends. Bancel, who had been unable to come, sent a long affectionate letter. In it he wrote:

. . . . Your life so far has been marked with great success, while mine has been about a failure. But fortunately I am not discouraged and one reason is that I have you as an example. It is a great comfort to me to know that I have you to turn to for advice.

You have all my love and sympathy; I have nothing else to give you except my friendship, which, of course, you have always had.

John was deeply touched by Bancel's letter. It showed the depth of his brother's humility. His mother's attitude had also changed. She had come to realize that John could not find true happiness as a parish priest. For all this understanding, John himself felt a momentary twinge of loneliness. From now on, he would no longer be part of his family, but of a community apart. Jesuit houses would be his home and he might be stationed anywhere. Still, he would be permitted to keep in touch with the family. Indeed this practice was encouraged.

John was not obliged to start at once his training for final acceptance into the Society. Still, as he said to Heinrich, "I believe when God calls it's safer to walk fast."

He applied for admission into the novitiate of the New York-Maryland Province of the Society, and his entrance was scheduled for November 13. As a novice he would continue his studies, teach, or do whatever was demanded of him by his superiors.

On the appointed day John arrived almost too late for the last train. To his horror, the gate was already closed and the conductor shouting, "All aboard."

Frantically, John yelled, "For heaven's sake, open the gate and let me through. I am *leaving the world* on this train and *must* make it!"

From the look of bewilderment on the conductor's face, John supposed later that the man thought he meant to take his own life. Still, he opened the gate. As John hurried through, he called back over one shoulder:

"Don't look so worried; everything's wonderful!"

6

Young Jesuit

DURING THE TESTING PERIOD before he should finally be accepted into the Society, John often thought what a small part his higher education had played in his present life. Making his bed, shining his shoes, and the endless other homely chores had little to do with theology or ancient civilizations. Such tasks could not be learned from books, and there were moments when he felt they could not be learned at all—at least by him!

Then he would say to Father Daniel Callahan, "You've been very patient. I imagine you're about ready to give me up."

Father Callahan had been assigned as a guide to help train John in the routine duties at the Jesuit Residence. A novice-priest like himself, Callahan had lived there longer and "knew the ropes." Not only this, he was practical and efficient. John couldn't imagine that he had ever had trouble arranging a bedspread so it wasn't all wrinkled, or found it difficult to put a uniform shine on his shoes.

Sometimes Daniel could not hide his amazement at his charge's clumsiness when attempting simple chores. "You've got to learn to use your hands as well as your head," he would often say. And toward this end he was strict taskmaster.

Once in a while, John was tempted to explain that he had always been poor at manual work, but he remained silent. Here, no one was interested in excuses. What he didn't do well he would have to learn. Perhaps, John hoped, this wouldn't be impossible. After all, he had trained his fingers to play the piano fairly well; so surely he could be trained to do domestic work—or, could he? He had never been able to make a Spencerian D.

John mentioned this humorously to Daniel one day. It was during a recreation period and the two were taking a brief walk on the grounds of the Residence. Aside from their guide-pupil relation, Daniel was an understanding friend. He laughed, and seemed to find the episode very amusing.

"I must be a better teacher than Mr. Sisson," Daniel said. "Though I still wouldn't recommend you as a butler, you *are* improving."

John was grateful for even this guarded praise. Back on the job, he knew that Daniel would be strict again. This was in line with the general attitude at the novitiate. Novices were constantly reminded that they were there on trial. Even a job well done might have been done better, and the smallest error was taken as a sign that one might not be fit to become a Jesuit.

There were times when it almost seemed that a superior was going out of his way to discourage the newcomers. It was then that John thought that giving up all his worldly possessions had been far less painful than not answering when unjustly rebuked. Gradually, though, he came to understand the reasons for the strict rules and many regulations. To be a Jesuit implied total sacrifice. Humility must be learned in "the ordinary way," which applied to the smallest detail of daily living.

The rules were not designed to make the novices fit into a single mold. Indeed, each young man was encouraged in his own special talent. There was, however, no distinction made between the most talented and the least gifted member of the Order. This was why John thought that poor manual skills might keep him from becoming a Jesuit. Later, when called upon to "use his head," he became more confident.

Then it was Daniel who voiced some doubts, saying, "You have a much better mind than I, John."

Gradually, John found that a background of learning served him well. He could call upon the classics to enliven his sermons. All the novices were required to give sermons at various churches in the Province. John's first experience in the pulpit took place in the Catholic Chapel of the Hudson River State Mental Hospital. He was as nervous as an actor on opening night, though he managed not to show it.

At first there was little more stirring about than in most congregations. Suddenly, then, a patient stood up and wildly waved his arms. The priest was not certain whether to duck or run. Fortunately, there was no need to do either. The man was merely showing his approval. He shouted heartily, "Grand work, old boy. Let's have more of it!"

This encouragement, John later revealed, made him sense his possibilities as a preacher.

Further contacts with mentally disturbed patients convinced John that many of these people could find deep comfort through prayer. Some patients told him that visits to the chapel had started them on the way back to sanity. Others found comfort in the confessional. These were people who, dwelling too much on sin, had forgotten God's love and forgiveness. These patients, seemingly so hopeless, could often be reached with a little understanding. This was equally true in all relations, John decided. Love can cast out fear and suspicion.

In the second year of his noviceship, young Father LaFarge was sent to teach at Loyola College in Baltimore. There he enjoyed working with the boys and encouraged an exchange of views between the students and himself. This method seemed to work, and John saw a future for himself in imparting knowledge to the young.

Soon after, he and Daniel Callahan were admitted as full-fledged members of the Society. Before being assigned to special work, both received permission to resume their studies toward a master of arts degree. John was overjoyed. He decided to take up philosophy and theology again. Refresher courses would aid him greatly in his teaching. Thus, in July of 1908, two soft-spoken Jesuits were seated on a train bound for Woodstock, Maryland. Although addressing one another as "Father LaFarge" and "Father Callahan," their conversation showed that they were friends of long standing. In their thoughts they were "John" and "Daniel," but in public, formality was the custom.

It was curious, John thought, how much one could change in a few years. Separation from worldly contacts made even a train ride seem a new experience. He felt shy about the passengers, who belonged to the other world that he had left. Only Daniel seemed personally related. Did he feel this way, too?

John gazed at his friend, who looked perfectly at ease in their surroundings—not strange, not shy. Daniel smiled and matter-of-factly said, "We'll be in Woodstock in about half an hour. This is what you've been waiting for, Father LaFarge."

"Yes, I have so very much to learn," John said.

"We both do," Daniel replied, but indifferently.

This was to dampen his own eagerness, John decided. Daniel did not completely agree with John's drive to learn more and more.

"Sooner or later, you're going to have to deal with people," he often said. This had a familiar sound to Father LaFarge. He had been given such advice or something like it ever since he had started to school.

Daniel again took up the theme. "Knowledge is fine," he said, "but when it comes to study, you're inclined to overdo."

John didn't deny this. When pursuing a subject, he found it difficult to stop. Still, wanting to reassure his friend, he said, "I shall try to lead a well-balanced life."

They noticed then that they were coming into Woodstock and took their bags down from the rack. As they stepped onto the platform, they were amazed to see a light snowfall. This was very rare for Maryland in July. Father Callahan smiled. "This is what I call a cold reception," he said.

But it would have taken more than a freak snow-storm to put down John's spirits. The road ahead seemed rosy. Here, in the lovely Maryland country-side, he would be working with Jesuit professors fa-mous in their special fields of knowledge. Perhaps someday he would also be a specialist.

Those two years at Woodstock did prove the most satisfying John had ever known. Neither Harvard nor Innsbruck had held such challenge. At Woodstock, subjects were taught in a way to make one seek fur-ther, and John soon forgot his promise to lead a "well-balanced life."

During the second summer, students and professors together traveled to St. Mary's County in Maryland. There they would spend a three-week vacation in a Jesuit Residence called the "Villa."

"Now that examinations are over, you can relax," Father Daniel told John. "If you don't mind my saying so, you're looking a bit seedy."

John insisted that he was in tiptop condition, but soon he discovered that he wasn't. Instead of benefit-ing from outdoor life, he felt fatigued most of the time. At first, Father Daniel tried to lure his friend from the couch by suggesting a swim in St. Mary's River. John joined him, but the result was a chill. After that, he begged off from outdoor activities. Father Daniel didn't insist, but said, "I warned you not to study too hard."

"I know," John said. "I know."

After returning to Woodstock, John did not feel much better. Though he was not allowed to do any chores, he could not relax. It almost seemed as if his examinations were still ahead of him.

Thus, one day after receiving a message that the Rector wished to see him, John felt a wave of anxiety. Perhaps the exam papers had been mixed up and he hadn't even passed! This was absurd, and he knew it; but on the way down the corridor John felt small beads of sweat on his brow.

Facing the Rector, he steadied himself on a chair.

"Sit down, John," his Superior said. "I must say you're not looking well at all."

John admitted that he had been under the weather, but thought that his health had improved somewhat.

He hoped so, the Rector said, for he had disturbing news. John's father was dying in a hospital in New York. He supposed John would wish to visit him.

"Of course," John said. He would like to leave at once. He was grateful for being permitted to do so.

The train seemed to make endless and unnecessary stops. If his father was so gravely ill, John feared he might not arrive on time. When reaching the hospital, however, he found his father conscious and alert. Margaret, his father explained, had gone to Newport to get the house in readiness for his return. He was happy to see his son, the artist said, and pleased that John had come.

His father spoke about his most recent work, a stained glass window representing the four law-givers—Moses, Socrates, Mohammed, and Emperor Justinian. He also mentioned his plans for the future, but in a way to make John feel that his father knew he did not have a future. He was extremely weak and often had to stop to catch his breath.

After a period of prolonged gasping, the artist said weakly, "Since you cannot stay, John, will you send me an understanding priest?"

John promised that he would. He supposed his father might be troubled about his past way of life. Since his standards had been different from most men's, he would need a wise confessor.

A few weeks later, Father LaFarge was roused from sleep by the Rector, and was told of his father's death. Though the news did not come as a surprise, John was shaken nonetheless.

The great artist was buried with a Solemn High Mass and laid to rest in the LaFarge vault in Greenwood Cemetery, Brooklyn.

Before returning to Woodstock, John stopped at the

Episcopal Church of the Ascension on Fifth Avenue. Along with other people in the pews, he gazed up at the enormous painting of the Ascension by his father. The mystical quality of this work impressed him deeply, and he thought that in spite of his father's unusual way of life, God would not judge him harshly. Like Christ, he too had no use for hypocrites. Besides, he had believed that all men were "children of the common Father."

Back in Woodstock, Father LaFarge tried in every way to improve his health. He took long walks designed to make him sleep. Instead, he merely became so tired that he tossed all night in bed. His present sorrow seemed to merge with every sorrow he had ever known. He had nightmares about sad partings and dreamed of the iron stove in the Newport nursery. There were no flames flickering behind the small isinglass panes . . . only darkness; and when John awoke, he did not feel like himself. He even found it difficult to pray, and knew that his nervousness was being noticed. He was therefore not surprised to be summoned again by the Rector.

"You'll have to do something about yourself, John," his superior announced bluntly. "Perhaps you and I should talk about what's bothering you most."

John admitted that he had overworked. Later, the

news of his father's illness had come. Ever since, he had been troubled by a sense of guilt. He felt this may have been because he was not present when his father died.

Gently the Rector probed into John's past, asking questions about his boyhood in relation to his father. Gradually, it became clear that John's guilt stemmed from the past. It was caused by a double feeling about his father. Along with his great admiration for the artist, he had also resented him, and would have preferred a father "like Mr. Hill."

Such emotions had been perfectly natural, the Rector said. It was not that John had ever lacked love for his father, but he had been deeply hurt by him. "And now that you've faced up to this," he said, "the guilt will go. While you're here, there is more," the Rector said, "for us to discuss."

He believed that much of John's poor health had been caused by overstudy, and he was extremely doubtful about his pursuing a purely intellectual life at this time.

"I've discussed this with the Father Provincial," the Rector said, "and we're in complete agreement."

Instead of protesting, John felt relieved that the decision had been made for him. He wondered what the Rector had in mind.

"Before anything else, you must rest," he told John. Arrangements had already been made for him to spend a few weeks at St. Thomas Manor, in Maryland.

"Then?" John asked excitedly.

Then, instead of going back to his books, it was felt that Father LaFarge would benefit by a life among people.

John packed up his few belongings, and a few books and manuscripts. The Seminary's delivery wagon carried these to the railroad station at the foot of the hill. A small Good-bye party gathered in John's room, headed by Father Callahan. In the middle of well-wishings, John suddenly realized that his only pair of respectable trousers had been packed. He made a frantic dash down the hill, pulled his trousers from the small trunk and rushed up the hill again. Father Daniel joined him on the final sprint to catch his train.

"You couldn't have run that fast a few weeks ago," he panted approvingly.

Though Father Daniel made no mention of the trouser near-mishap, John knew what he was thinking. As he waved from the platform, Father Daniel's expression seemed to say: "You'll learn, my absent-minded professor pupil, that life is more than learning."

After leaving St. Thomas Manor, John was transferred to Old St. Joseph's Church in Philadelphia. This familiar city brought back many memories of his boyhood—happy memories now, and totally without guilt. After several weeks of peaceful work in Philadelphia, he was sent to Blackwells Island, an isolated spot in New York Harbor that contained the State Penitentiary and New York City Hospital. The only way to reach the island was by a small ferry boat from the foot of East 72nd Street in Manhattan. Evidently he was now considered well enough to face life in the raw.

Father LaFarge's duties were to assist Father John Casey, who was the chaplain in charge of three institutions: the City Home, the Work House, and the Metropolitan, which was a hospital on the north end of the island. John was installed in the Work House, where he was provided with a roomy study and an adjoining bedroom. There was no chapel in the Work House, but he celebrated Mass in the hall upstairs.

Those first nights inside prison walls were very frightening. The only light was an electric bulb shining through a transom. The prisoners in their cell blocks seemed dangerous. Later, though, when he was called upon to help them Father LaFarge again decided that differences could be bridged by under-

*Many of these people had known nothing
but misery.*

standing. To give some small hope to these derelicts brought him close to God in a different way than by prayer and study. In contrast to his own background of culture and comfort, many of these people had known nothing but misery. When he prayed with them, they no longer felt that they were forgotten.

Indeed, it was there in the tuberculosis ward that Father LaFarge heard a statement of faith never topped in any book. Old John Lennon, who had only 32¢ to his name, had lain ill for four years on the top floor of the dreary building. When the priest called, Old John was usually full of wise-cracks and bits of information. This day, though, he seemed serious.

"Tell me, Father," he said, "why does God seem to treat people so unequally?"

The priest supposed that Old John was going to complain about his bitter lot. Instead, the old man answered his own question. "Many of the rich folks on Fifth Avenue might have a lot of trouble staying out of hell. But a poor sinner like me has been given grace and the hope of heaven—seems more than I deserve."

Father LaFarge smiled. Amen, he said to himself.

After that, it didn't seem to matter anymore where he might be sent next. Someday, perhaps, he might again pursue that intellectual life. Now, he actually preferred a life of sharing.

7

The Ridge

FOR THE PAST FOUR YEARS Father LaFarge had been assistant pastor at St. Aloysius Church in Leonardtown, Maryland. This was one of a string of Jesuit missions that had been settled long ago on a strip of land between the Chesapeake Bay and the St. Mary's River. This area, known locally as "The Ridge," was difficult to reach. For this reason it had not kept up with the times. Indeed, it sometimes seemed that the people's attitudes had changed very little from those of the early English Catholics who had emigrated to America with the second Lord Baltimore. No one seemed to mind that modern cities had not pushed close with the improvements they might have brought into this backwoods country.

Father LaFarge had just returned from a distant sick call. He went into the small library, where he and the pastor, Father Lawrence Kelly, wrote their sermons, chatted, relaxed, or read. The younger priest struck a match and lighted a small oil lamp that cast a soft glow in the room. As familiar objects appeared within the circle of light, Father LaFarge felt a pang of regret. The following week he would be transferred to another mission.

It wasn't wise for a Jesuit to become too much attached to any place, Father LaFarge thought. Nor should one become too fond of people. Still, he had made many close friends here, and he would miss Father Kelly. As assistant pastor he had varied and endless duties. Besides daily Mass, baptizing and other church activities, he had also made many a visit to the homes of his scattered flock.

The parish extended for miles, and one had to travel over almost impassable roads to reach some of the people. Father LaFarge often thought that many of his charges would have been neglected had it not been for the horse and buggy. It was a good thing, he admitted more than once, that his loyal, hardworking horse often knew the way better than he.

These reflections were interrupted by Father Kelly, who just then came into the study. The pastor was an energetic young man, who affectionately regarded his assistant as a dreamer. He seated himself and suggested that the two should have a talk.

Father Kelly rarely spoke in personal terms, but now he was about to break this rule.

"I'm sorry to see you leave," the pastor said, "and all the parishioners feel the same. You have a gift for people, John, but before you go, I'd like to give you a little advice."

"Your suggestions are always welcome," John said.

"From what I've heard about your new assignment," Father Kelly said, "you'll have your hands full." Not that John had ever shirked his duties, the pastor added swiftly; only that at St. Inigoes he would be faced with many complex problems. The new assistant should not expect to work wonders in too short a time. People were slow to change, and many did not practice what they preached. He deeply admired John's efforts in behalf of the Negroes, but he might run into opposition if he pushed too hard.

Father LaFarge looked up sharply at that, but said nothing.

"I don't mean that you shouldn't keep on trying, John," Father Kelly added. "But don't expect to get rid of bigotry on The Ridge with a few sermons."

Father LaFarge knew that this was sound advice. Here on The Ridge, the white folks' attitude toward the Negroes was inherited from the old days of slavery. Indeed, most of the Negroes were descendants of slaves who had been bonded to old manor houses in the community. Now they labored as farmhands, fishermen, and oystermen part of the year, tending their own small patches of ground for the rest.

"What moves me," Father LaFarge said, "is the patience of these people. They make so few claims to their rightful freedoms."

"I know," Father Kelly said, "but it's hard to change men's hearts. Try to be patient, John."

His assistant promised that he should certainly try.

Early the following morning, Father LaFarge drove off in his buggy. The air was chill with a touch of frost, but a preheated brick at his feet kept him warm. He decided to visit some parishioners on the outer fringe of the parish, then work his way back toward evening. If he were detained he could always sleep in one of the homes along the way. A priest was always welcome, even in the humblest shanties. Wealthy families in manors and plantations kept a special "priest's room" for those who might wish to stop.

He came to a curve in the road that rounded a patch of swampland. Swerving off a rut might well have landed him in the mud. Soon, though, he was on an even stretch again and then he spied a familiar figure. Her name was Mrs. Mary Jones but she was commonly called Aunt Pigeon. She moved to the side when he drove up. The priest pulled on the reins and called, "Climb in and ride along with me."

Aunt Pigeon hoisted herself into the buggy, with remarkable ease for a woman who claimed to be one hundred and six years old.

"What are you doing in these parts?" Father La-Farge asked.

Aunt Pigeon explained that she had been given a "lift" from her parish and was going to visit some distant relatives—the Jenks family. Mrs. Jenks was a great-niece of her second cousin. The priest must know them, she pattered on.

"I know them very well," Father LaFarge said. He was especially fond of the third son, Jeb, an unusually bright little fellow. But before he had time to say so, Aunt Pigeon was off on another subject.

She had heard that Father was about to move to her parish at St. Inigoes. This, she said, pleased her very much. She didn't hold with the priest who was leaving; his sermons were too short. It was her view that if people traveled many miles to Mass, they deserved to get their money's worth.

This reminded her of other priests, some that she "held with" and others she didn't. Aunt Pigeon plunged into the past. She rambled on about the old slave days—how she and the other little Negro girls had walked eight miles to Mass. They had gone barefoot, carrying their linen dresses wrapped in bundles. When nearing the church, they had hidden in the woods, put on their shoes and stockings and white dresses. On the way home they reversed the process.

Somehow, her treble chatter reminded Father LaFarge of Nonna—his Grandmother Perry—whose life had been one of refinement and ease. When Nonna had called up her ancestors, they emerged with generations of culture in the background. The white man's sin of slavery, Father LaFarge thought, had given the Negro small chance to build any kind of culture.

He asked Aunt Pigeon how she had managed to keep so lively and cheerful at her age.

"That's simple," she said. "All one has to do is love God and dance."

She explained that the name Pigeon had been given to her in childhood because she danced the Pigeon Wing. With that her mood changed suddenly.

"I always say, the darker the night, the brighter you've got to shine," she added.

The priest decided that this was to let him know that she had also had her hardships.

About a quarter of a mile farther on, they came to her relatives' house. Father LaFarge decided he would also stop to visit the Jenkses. The place was alive with neighboring children, who should have been in school. Most Negroes, though, did not attend class for more than two months in the year. Many of their teachers had not even studied beyond the fourth grade.

The priest's arrival was followed by hearty-voiced, friendly greetings. Soon he was surrounded by the children, and Mrs. Jenks could scarcely make herself heard above the din. Her husband, she managed to say, would be disappointed to have missed the priest. But he was an oysterman, and he had to work down at the shore. Then she interrupted herself to say, "Bless us—I almost forgot! Could I make you something to eat, Father? You've had a long trip."

Since he had already breakfasted, Father LaFarge accepted only a cup of chicory before going on his way. As the youngsters plied him with questions, he noticed that Jeb was not among them. "Where's young Jeb?" he asked.

"Oh, he flew out the back door when he saw you coming, Father," the mother said. "He was feared to see you. He's been bad."

"I'm sure he hasn't been that bad; please call him in, won't you?"

Mrs. Jenks shouted through the rear door, and her reluctant son appeared. Eyes downcast and shame-faced, he shifted from foot to foot.

"How is my friend Jeb?" Father LaFarge asked.

There was no reply, only silence and turning away.

In gentle tones, the priest coaxed Jeb to come closer, then raised the boy's chin with a fingertip. Somehow, as if sensitive to the scene, the other children formed a silent tableau at the far end of the room.

"What is it, Jeb—what have you done?"

"Tell him," Jeb's mother said, nudging him sharply. "Go get your book and show Father what you've done."

The boy produced a picture book that Father La-Farge had given him on an earlier visit. He had found such "visual-aids" helpful to a better understanding of religion.

"Jeb scribbled all over the Lord," his mother said, sounding quite alarmed.

Father LaFarge opened to a page where the face and hands of Christ had been blackened with a bit of charcoal.

"Tain't scribbling," Jeb muttered. "Tain't scribbling at all."

The priest understood at once. Jeb had not meant to deface the book, but, rather, to come closer to Christ by making him a black man.

"Look at me, Jeb," he said. When Jeb returned his gaze, the priest went on softly—just between the two,

"It was hot in the land where our Lord lived, and I'm sure his skin was deeply browned by the sun."

Jeb broke into a radiant smile and exclaimed to the room at large, "See, that's how I hoped it was!"

"But I don't want you marking up the book, Jeb. Just remember that God does not judge people by the color of their skin."

St. Inigoes Manor was located at the mouth of the St. Inigoes Creek, where it joined the St. Mary's River. The Jesuit Residence had been built in traditional Colonial style, with a spacious central hallway. Instead of being a classic example of the period, though, the house had a lopsided look. This was because one of the wings had been destroyed by fire. The house now consisted only of a few rooms and a chapel, which had been added on at a later date. The lawn was shaded by handsome pecan trees planted by the early missionaries. There was also a fig tree laden with fruit at the gate of the Residence.

When Father LaFarge arrived, the St. Inigoes community consisted of Father Matthews, the superior, and Father Emerick, who had been a missionary in Jamaica, British West Indies. Although they were assigned different tasks, they helped one another out when necessary. Often they were so busy with their own special duties that they met only at meals, which were served in the housekeeper's frame cottage near the Residence.

Father LaFarge's first assignment was to restore St. James Church, which was sorely needed in the community. This plain box-like structure had previously been used as a parish center and entertainment hall. It was separated from the Residence by a dense forest. After the place was made habitable, Father LaFarge conducted Mass and other services there, and planned various programs for the parishioners.

All in all, the new priest had a warm welcome. Yet at the very start he was confronted by a whole array of new problems. Many of these resulted from prejudice between various ethnic groups. "Keeping the Negro in his place" was the general attitude of the white folk. But then, among the whites the Slavic colony—most of whom were Czechs and Slovaks—were considered inferior by the English, who had been longer on the land.

With all their differences, there was a spirit of unity about putting the church into condition. The Slavs got together and helped clear the land. Soon a new barn, with a corn crib on top, sheltered the horse and buggy. One far-sighted parishioner donated a black snake. This was put into the corn crib to discourage rats and other petty thieves that might be tempted to gnaw on the kernels.

Rufus Hughes, an elderly, long-bearded Negro, had a gift for discovering water. He padded around barefoot till he found a spot where he felt that a well should be dug. At a place where two lines of vegetation crossed, he insisted that water would be abundant. And Rufus's prophecy proved to be correct.

But when the time came to plan church activities and programs, this spirit of unity did not prevail. Each group made suggestions about how things should be run. The early Ridge settlers felt that they should be first consulted. They were full of advice. Father LaFarge should know, the English settlers warned, that the Slavs were strange people who had never lost their foreignness. In fact, if the priest didn't prevent it, these latecomers would try to introduce Old Country ways. Politely, he tried to reassure everybody. It was his hope that everyone would be happy at St. James.

Shortly after the church was ready for use, Henry Johnson, the Negro sexton, announced that Father LaFarge had a caller. He was Mr. Kohut, Henry said, shaking his head as if he expected trouble.

Since the sexton was usually meek and unruffled, Father LaFarge wondered why he now had an anxious air. He himself had frequently met Mr. Kohut, the robust leader of the Slavic group, and had not found him alarming in the least. He tried to convey this by saying, "Mr. Kohut is a splendid worker, Henry."

"No denyin' him that," the sexton replied. "He's more like a steam engine on legs than a man."

Because there was something apt about this description, the priest did not reply. He turned to hide a smile and moved from the small sacristy into the church. There his visitor was stomping up and down the aisle. He greeted the priest in booming tones, then went on to voice the reason for his visit.

He wanted to talk about seating arrangements in the church, Mr. Kohut began, without ceremony. Perhaps the priest didn't know that his people were against mixing the men and women during worship. It was their custom for the men to sit together and likewise the women. Also, boys were supposed to sit with boys and girls with girls. This was how it had to be.

It was taken for granted by both Slavs and early settlers that Negroes would be confined to their own section.

At any rate, after weeks of practice and many mix-ups, people managed to find their places in the church. Then Mr. Kohut made another suggestion. The Slavs should be permitted to sing hymns in their own language. These hymns were melodious and might have been well-received, if it hadn't been for their leader, Mr. Kohut himself. As Father LaFarge told his superior, "Mr. Kohut sings with the fervor of an angel and the voice of a foghorn."

Sometimes these petty prejudices seemed a small reflection of what was happening in the world. The intense national rivalries John had noticed at Innsbruck were now threatening to cause a war that might engulf all mankind. Here on the Ridge this still seemed quite remote. In his own small way Father LaFarge tried to promote brotherhood by bringing about a better spirit of cooperation among his own people.

On the second and fourth Sunday of every month, he boarded a boat at the wharf and sailed across the river to St. George's Island. There, on this low-lying tract of wooded land, he would say Mass on Monday morning. This journey often brought back scenes of his childhood, and St. Mary's River was transformed into Narragansett Bay. Briefly, he was again a boy in Newport, and it saddened him to think that the concept of home and family had been weakened in many parts of the world.

Men were being taught to look to a cold, unloving State for comfort. This idea stemmed from the Bolshevik revolution, now spread far beyond the boundaries of Russia. Even here, in the backwoods of Maryland, hate leaflets were sometimes handed out in Longmore's General Store. Their aim was to sow discord among the Negroes.

In 1915 the great English liner *Lusitania* was sunk by a German submarine off the Irish coast, and many American passengers were lost. In 1917 the United States declared war against Germany, and her young men sailed for foreign shores "to make the world safe for democracy," as President Wilson promised.

Meanwhile, Father LaFarge went about his ordinary tasks. He hoped in some small way to aid the future cause of peace, by promoting tolerance. He wanted also to do his best to preserve the ideals set down by the Founding Fathers. Without education the underprivileged would always be a prey to alien ideas. Democracy must practice what it preached— the chance of equality for all. In this backwoods of Maryland, one of the greatest needs was for better education.

Father LaFarge met with no great difficulties in establishing a new school for the white children. Classes were conducted in the church, where on weekdays a large canvas curtain was let down in front of the altar. Finally, with much persistence and pleading, he obtained funds to start a school for the Negro children.

From the first, heaven seemed to smile upon this venture. He was fortunate in finding an ideal teacher, Mrs. Jennie Beale. She had attended a convent school

conducted by colored sisters, and was firm in her belief that Negro boys and girls could learn quickly if given a chance.

Together Father LaFarge and Mrs. Beale set a date for the opening, and this was announced throughout the parish. Eagerly the priest awaited the day when his fondest dream would be realized. After saying Mass and taking care of his parish duties, he decided to go and see how Mrs. Beale was doing. The weather was terrible, with rain falling from the skies in sheets. He was happy, though, as he sloshed on through the mud.

When he arrived at the school house, he found Mrs.

When Father LaFarge arrived at the schoolhouse,
he found Mrs. Beale with a solitary student.

Beale with only one student. Undaunted, she was addressing her solitary charge as if the classroom were full. Nor did the small boy seated there turn when Father LaFarge came in. It was the teacher who spied him and announced that class would be recessed for a few moments. She turned to the priest then and said, "Don't worry, Father. A good thing started is bound to grow."

With far less assurance, he replied, "Of course, Mrs. Beale, of course."

He glanced at the lone figure seated behind a desk and was greeted by a shy smile on the face of young Jeb Jenks. Not wanting to interfere with regulations, Father LaFarge asked permission to speak to the boy. This granted, he said, with a question in his voice, "Well, Jeb, you're a long way from your own parish, aren't you?"

Jeb explained he was now living with kinfolk of Aunt Pigeon so that he could go to school. Because learning was so important to all the Jenks family, his mother had agreed to this arrangement.

"Anyhow," he added, "I wanted to belong to this parish, because you are my friend."

"We are indeed good friends," Father LaFarge said.

Not only did this first school thrive, but, in the following years, more schools sprang up in parishes all over the Ridge. In a ceaseless effort to gain better education for the people, Father LaFarge became a beggar for his cause.

Gradually the need for education in the rural districts became a public concern. Father LaFarge was no longer a lonely pioneer. A bill was passed by the Maryland Legislature to provide an industrial school in the counties of the State. This offer of State funds combined with church and community money was an answer to the priest's most fervent prayers.

The Cardinal Gibbons Institute was thus born—a place where young men and women could be trained in manual skills. There were also to be programs to instruct local farmers, both Negro and white, about modern methods for growing their crops.

In spite of Government funds, more money was needed to maintain the Institute. The Executive Committee, which was based in New York, included men of all races and creeds and was headed by Father LaFarge's brother Oliver.

Fund-raising attempts were often discouraging in the results. These were the Depression years. Besides, Father LaFarge discovered that far too few Northerners were interested in the Negroes' plight in the South. Still, the priest often thought, there were men whose devotion matched his own. One of these was George K. Hunton, and Father's cousin Schuyler N. Warren, who had brought these two men together. As the secretary of the Executive Committee, Mr. Hunton labored endlessly to raise funds and to interest people in the Institute.

Though it lasted for only a few years, the Cardinal Gibbons Institute became a model for similar schools all over the country. Furthermore, a seed had been planted that grew and flowered. The work done at the Institute aroused the interest of many Catholic leaders in the problems of the Negro. These far-reaching results so inspired Father LaFarge that he started to write articles on the subject. These articles dealt with strengthening the forces of democracy and they were well-received. The Jesuit magazine *America* showed interest in his gift for writing.

Those years had been hectic—a struggle all the way. Sometimes Father LaFarge suspected that he might have pushed too hard. But, then, through the grace of God and hard work, Mrs. Beale's promise had come true:

"A good thing started is bound to grow!"

8

Interracial Justice

AFTER FIFTEEN YEARS on the Ridge, the great world beyond it seemed remote to Father LaFarge. He felt as though he had settled there for good; indeed, he had no wish for it to be otherwise. Then in 1925 he received a telegram from his sister Margaret, saying that their mother was gravely ill. He left at once for Newport, and when he arrived there, the reunion with his family made it seem as though they had never parted.

His dear sister Emily was not there, however. She had died a few years before. All the others had assembled at their mother's bedside. She was very weak and suffering. In spite of this, she joked about the many people in attendance. It was quite a crowd, Margaret LaFarge said, with day nurses and night nurses and members of the family.

Shortly before her death, Margaret LaFarge seemed to see something that gave her great joy. Her expression as she died, John thought, had the tranquil look of a soul happily united with God.

That night the brothers and sisters sat together for the first time in many years. They were curiously light-hearted, for this was what their mother would have wanted.

"Death," she had always said, "is a natural thing like birth and growth and old age. When it comes, it will be familiar and welcome."

After the funeral Mass at St. Mary's, Margaret La-Farge was buried in St. Columba's Cemetery, a few miles outside of Newport. Later on the same day, Father LaFarge received a telephone call from his former pastor, Father Kelly, who was now the Provincial of the Jesuits in New York. After expressing regret about the mother's death, Father Kelly asked his old assistant pastor to stop in New York before he returned to the Ridge. The editor of *America*, Father Wilfred Parsons, had some things he wished to discuss. John supposed this might have to do with future articles. Instead, when he stopped at Campion House, Father Parsons invited him to join the staff of *America*.

In some surprise, Father LaFarge explained that if he were to leave the Ridge abruptly, it would upset plans at the Cardinal Gibbons Institute, and so he pleaded for a postponement. His request was granted.

A year later, however, Father LaFarge received word that he had been appointed to the staff of *America*. There was no arguing this time. Though his new assignment sounded interesting, he was heavy-hearted about leaving the Ridge. The faces of his old friends could not conceal their sadness. He would miss those familiar faces; but he was again reminded that the life of a Jesuit is determined by God's plan and not his own.

On the day of his departure Father LaFarge suddenly recalled that Jeb Jenks, in his teens now and a graduate of Cardinal Gibbons Institute, had not been one of the well-wishers who had come to say Farewell. From the train window, the priest gazed out at the people waving from the platform. Apart from the group and in the rear was Jeb. He stood alone, unable to raise an arm in a gesture of farewell, and finally he turned away abruptly so that no one would see him weep.

For fifteen years Father LaFarge had lived in a rural community where people spoke to one another even though they had never met. Now in New York he walked the city streets unnoticed by passers-by. Children here looked like the children in the country, but they and he were strangers.

At first, life seemed lonely in the city, but soon Father LaFarge became interested in his work. His regular routine was to compose a weekly column called "With Scrip and Staff." Many readers responded to his column by writing letters. This gave the priest a sense of conversing with people.

Besides, Father LaFarge decided that there was no reason why people on the streets should be strangers. A spirit of friendliness could overcome that. His habit of smiling at passers-by did not go unnoticed. The new editor-in-chief, Father Francis X. Talbot, called in his green assistant to give him a bit of advice.

"Remember, you're in the city now, John," he said. "There are all kinds of people roaming about. Don't be too trusting."

Father LaFarge by now had become accustomed to advice. Usually these warnings concerned his un-worldliness. True, he did such things as packing his only pair of decent trousers—and he had been known to go into a restaurant for a cup of coffee and discover that he had no money to pay for it. . . .

Father Talbot was speaking again.

"Remember," he said, "St. Christopher will be of absolutely no protection if you continue to ignore traffic signals. It's worth life and limb to cross the streets with you."

The cub-editor promised to try to mend his ways.

On matters other than his absent-mindedness, Father LaFarge was treated with respect. His opinion was often asked about matters relating to the magazine, and his suggestions were often followed. His own column was sometimes light and sometimes serious. Always, though, his point of view was strictly American. His message to the unseen audience was one of democracy. To improve the lot of underprivileged people was his aim.

He became interested in a movement now called the National Catholic Rural Life Conference. This great work had grown out of the efforts of a priest in Iowa, Luigi Ligutti, to help the farmers of his neighborhood through a period of severe depression. And when Father LaFarge was sent to "cover" the meetings of the Rural Life Conference, he and Father Ligutti became firm, lifelong friends, bound in a common cause.

From the Cardinal Gibbons Institute Father LaFarge had learned how a rural-minded priest could help the people by putting them in touch with Government and State aid. This was of course especially true of Negroes, who were not only affected by poor economic conditions in the community, but also by prejudice against the color of their skin.

"Someday soon," Father LaFarge told his editor, "I'm going to start an interracial group."

"Meantime," Father Talbot suggested quietly, "How about doing some writing on the subject?"

All in all, Father LaFarge was kept very busy. But,

his contact with small-town people, whose earnings stemmed from the soil, was a bridge between the bucolic life on the Ridge and the hectic pace of the city.

In 1938 Father LaFarge was sent to the International Eucharistic Congress in Budapest. Because of his familiarity with many languages, it was felt that he could more readily communicate with foreign delegates than any other member of the staff.

Father LaFarge welcomed this opportunity to travel. From an editorial point of view, it was a great advantage to learn first-hand about the regimes of Hitler and Mussolini. Many Americans could not bring themselves to believe that these dictators should be taken seriously.

His first stop was in England, where he met Miss Annie O'Brien Christitch, a part-Serbian, part-Irish correspondent for *America*. She told him that the English people were not so worried about the possibility of war as those in the United States. They felt that the dictators could be handled somehow.

When she learned that he was about to leave for Czechoslovakia, Miss Christitch arranged a meeting for Father LaFarge with Jan Masaryk, the son of the famous founder and first president of the unhappy country. The younger Mr. Masaryk, the country's foreign minister, received Father LaFarge alone and poured out his fears that his country would soon be invaded by the Germans. Their fate, he knew, would be the same as that of Austria, where Hitler's storm troopers were already entrenched. In that country, Socialists, Catholics, Jews, and peasants were being imprisoned or slaughtered by the Gestapo.

"If the British stand by their commitments to my country," Masaryk went on, "I shall urge my people to fight."

Father LaFarge decided to spend a week in Paris before resuming his trip to Budapest. A visit at the Jesuit headquarters there might give him a better perspective on the invasion "jitters." The Parisians' view of the situation was typically French. Hitler was a *gauche* paperhanger, they would say with a shrug; no one should take him seriously. Besides, what did the French have to fear? If Hitler was stupid enough to try to invade their country, he would be turned back at the Maginot Line.

From France Father LaFarge boarded a train for Germany, bound for Coblenz, to spend a few days with his old Innsbruck classmate, Dr. Heinrich Chardon. As the train neared the border, passengers grew scarce and the priest's spirits sank at the thought of entering Hitler's land.

Once beyond the border, his compartment was empty except for a solitary man. When the priest tried to talk to him, the passenger looked terrified. It was evidently dangerous for Germans to be seen talking to the clergy. So as not to cause further alarm, Father LaFarge gazed out the window.

As they approached Coblenz, the countryside grew lovelier. The quaint little villages reminded Father LaFarge of small houses around a Christmas tree. It became colder and darker in the long twilight of Northern Europe. As the train drew up to one of the villages, the priest saw a roadside shrine. Newly carved in wood stood a statue of the Blessed Virgin. A few candles burned at her feet. Brave hands had held those candles, Father LaFarge reflected.

In Coblenz Father Chardon introduced the American visitor to his parishioners. Father LaFarge was greeted warmly and pelted with questions. Where had he come from? the people wanted to know. When he told them he had left Paris that morning, they couldn't believe that it was true.

"And you are still safe?" they questioned in chorus.

They had been told that the streets of Paris were running with blood, and that the citizens were being murdered by Jews and Bolsheviks.

Father LaFarge assured them that he had crossed

the Place de la Concorde in a taxi on the way to the station. He had seen nothing except a few delivery boys on bicycles—no signs of bloodshed or revolution.

It did not take long to learn that the German people were kept in total ignorance of everything that was going on. In Coblenz you could not learn what was happening in Bonn or Cologne. You could not write letters. Obviously you could not telephone, and it was dangerous to send messages. Out in the country on the following afternoon, he and Father Chardon watched the Hitler *Jugend*—young boys marching up and down in front of an old village church. Like wooden puppets these fair-haired children goose-stepped behind a pasty-faced young man who was discharging his duties to *Der Fuehrer*, Hitler.

Father LaFarge became more and more convinced that the Nazis intended to do away with all religion. This became even more apparent after he arrived in Budapest, for the Eucharistic Congress. There, pilgrims were streaming in from many lands to pay homage to Christ, but Germans and Austrians did not attend the Congress. Hitler had ordered them to stay away.

Nor did he find Fascist Italy any less disturbing. In his desire to restore the Roman Empire, Mussolini had sent his troops into Ethiopia. The emperor of Ethiopia,

Haile Selassie, had pleaded before the League of Nations, and his pleas had gone unheeded. The world had listened but would not intervene.

To foreign visitors it was pointed out how much the country of Italy had improved after Mussolini had become dictator. Indeed, some gains had been made on the surface, but the living conditions of the poor were as dismal as any Father LaFarge had ever seen. Also, the Fascists had adopted the Nazi's racist ideas. Minority groups, especially Jews, were being persecuted. And although Mussolini gave lip-service to the Church, he had no use for religion.

While Father LaFarge was in Rome he received a message from the Vatican. The Holy Father, it read, wished a private audience with the American visitor.

He was warmly received by Pope Pius XI, who spoke on many subjects. Chiefly, the Holy Father said, he wanted to discuss the question of racism, which was now a burning issue in Germany and Italy. The Pope told his American guest that he had read his book, *Interracial Justice,* and thought it was the best ever written on this topic.

Father LaFarge was astounded. As a matter of routine he had sent the Pope a copy of this book when it was off the press. That the Pope had read and approved the work was very gratifying.

Soon after his audience, Father LaFarge joined a group of Jesuits to listen to Hitler speak from the Sportspalast in Berlin. The Fuehrer's voice came loud and clear, and the full-throated roar from the massed audience: "Sieg Heil! Sieg Heil! Sieg Heil!"

Hitler then vented his hate against Eduard Benes. This Czechoslovakian leader was an aggressor, he declared. He was a tyrant, an enemy of the German people.

Surely, Father LaFarge thought, this shouting from the Sportspalast was the voice of impending war.

After the speech, the Father General rose abruptly and said, "I still have hope that there will be no war."

There was no war for the moment, because England and France signed a pact in Munich with Hitler.

When Father LaFarge returned to America, he expressed his doubts that peace could be maintained. And his doubts later proved to be well founded. The Munich Pact was merely a prelude to World War II. Hitler's troops invaded Czechoslovakia, then Poland, then Belgium and France.

Three years later, in 1941, America was drawn into the conflict by the bombing of Pearl Harbor.

The best way to serve his country, Father LaFarge thought, was to work against those forces that could weaken democracy. In Germany and Italy he had seen

men silenced because of fear. False rumors and racist
ideas had resulted in the imprisonment or execution of
millions of men and women—without even a trial.

As he had earlier become concerned with the welfare of the Negro, Father LaFarge was now convinced
that injustice toward any group was a threat to freedom for all. The magazine *America* must be truly
American, he resolved. His pen would plead for equality and justice. This, though, was not enough. He must
play a more active role.

For many years he had worked with others who also
were interested in bettering relations between the
races. Among these people were both clergymen and
lay people. As they discovered their common interests
they formed a group that became the Catholic Interracial Council. Something like this had been a dream of
Father LaFarge's and of George Hunton's since those
days on the Ridge. Father LaFarge often said that
without George Hunton nothing could have been accomplished. For his part Mr. Hunton insisted that Father LaFarge had always been the spirit behind the
movement.

George Hunton, as secretary of the Council, combined Irish idealism with Yankee practicality. "And a

good thing, too," this canny New Hampshire-born lawyer often remarked.

This was when he felt called upon to give Father LaFarge advice. When George got that Yankee look on his face, the priest would ask, "What have I done now?"

The usual answer was that Father was trying to go too fast.

"Funds," the lawyer would remind the priest. "As usual, we are out of funds."

In the end they always managed to scrape enough together to keep the work going.

By now, the Catholic Interracial Council had a permanent center, a suite of offices high up in an older office building at 20 Vesey Street, in lower Manhattan. At the center, people could receive all kinds of information on racial matters. To promote better understanding there were also weekly meetings for the members, both white and Negro, and their guests. Though held in a long conference room, the meetings were informal. Everyone was welcome, and encouraged to speak up in the discussion that followed the featured speaker—who might be a bishop from Africa, a Harlem judge, or a California schoolteacher.

One Thursday evening the speaker at the get-together was to be a member of the NAACP (National Association for the Advancement of the Colored People), who would discuss Negro legal rights. When Father LaFarge arrived at Vesey Street, George Hunton was already there, and deeply engaged in conversation with a young man whose slim silhouette seemed somehow familiar to Father LaFarge. When he entered, Mr. Hunton nodded and the visitor turned. The years were swept away, as Father LaFarge gazed into the genial face of Jeb Jenks!

Only a few people had arrived; so the two old friends had time for a few words. Jeb, it turned out, was visiting some of his wife's relatives in New York. He had just happened to come into the center for some information and met Mr. Hunton. When he learned that Father LaFarge would probably be coming, of course he had decided to stay.

Father LaFarge could scarcely believe that Jeb was married, and was living in Baltimore with his wife and young son.

"What about your work?" Father LaFarge asked.

Jeb said that his training at the Cardinal Gibbons Institute now stood him in good stead. He knew now that without manual skills it was difficult for Negroes to get decent jobs. He was working in a war plant, but expected to enlist in the Armed Forces soon.

The priest was eager to hear more about Jeb's son,

but the room had filled up and the meeting came to order.

The speaker explained the work of the NAACP, which advised Negroes of their legal rights. Many poor people living in the slums, he said, didn't even know there were laws to protect them against unfair practices. Such groups as the Catholic Interracial Council, he went on, served to enlighten people. The spirit here was a bridge toward better understanding.

The speaker went on to praise the devotion of Father LaFarge and George Hunton to the Negro cause. In the face of opposition, he said they had remained steadfast throughout the years.

His speech was followed by a lively give-and-take among the guests. Father LaFarge was enjoying the discussion thoroughly—here, he was thinking, was a spirit of fellowship at work—when suddenly a voice from a far corner of the room struck a note out of key with all that had gone before.

Angrily, a young Negro cried out, "And what are you gentlemen doing about our boys in the Army? Or haven't you seen blacks marching with blacks and whites marching with whites? Or didn't you know, if a black soldier gets thirsty down South, he can't drink from a public fountain. But he can die for his country. You people make me laugh!"

"There is truth in what you say, and cause for your

bitterness," Father LaFarge said quietly. True, there was still much to be accomplished. That was the reason for these Thursday meetings, and all the hard labor of the Interracial Council. But little could be gained through hate, and much through mutual effort.

His gentleness seemed only to provoke the young man further. Full of fury, he shouted, "And you—you priests—are the biggest hypocrites of all!"

This was not the first time Father LaFarge had been called names. Most of the time he didn't mind, and he did not now. Indeed, he felt sorry for the angry young man.

Someone else did mind, though. Jeb Jenks sprang to his feet, scarcely less angry than his opponent. But his tones were controlled as he said, "The trouble with men like you is you don't know a friend when you see one. You just want to think all white men feel the same. You don't want to get together. And I think it would be nice if you'd tell Father LaFarge you're sorry."

"Not me!"

The two young men advanced toward one another, fists clenched. It seemed there was bound to be a fight, but George Hunton intervened. Very firmly, he announced that if there was any trouble he would call in the police.

"You priests are the biggest hypocrites of all!"
the young man shouted.

The angry young man backed away and left the room muttering. Soon after, Father looked around for Jeb, but he also had disappeared.

The meeting gradually broke up, and Father La-Farge packed papers into his briefcase. He was saying Goodnight to George when a prosperous-looking white man suddenly loomed in front of him. His face was flushed and his eyes were narrowed to two angry slits.

"This meeting was a disgrace," the portly stranger bellowed. "I've been watching you, Father LaFarge. You're a trouble maker. How do you expect business-men like me to get along when you're always demand-ing higher salaries for the working men? I came here to see what this racial business was like, and believe you me, I saw! Nothing but a common brawl. I'm going to report you to the Cardinal."

Somewhat sharply, Father LaFarge replied, "Please do. It wouldn't be the first time." He paused then and added, "And I'll tell you what. Stop around at Cam-pion House tomorrow. I'll show you a letter from the Holy Father. He is very much interested in the work we're doing here."

"The Holy Father . . . what is the Church coming to!" the gentleman exclaimed. He turned on his heel and stalked out.

There was a brief silence, then George Hunton laughed aloud.

"Good for you, my friend," he said. "You almost lost your temper."

9

The Ordinary Way

FATHER LAFARGE sat behind a large rosewood desk that seemed just right for the ornate architecture of Campion House. He had inherited this handsome piece of furniture along with his new appointment as editor-in-chief of *America*. Another mark of his present rank was a large upholstered chair that could be swung about or tilted. But in spite of its splendor, the casters had a way of coming off. When this happened, the tall editor-in-chief was reduced to crawling on all fours to find them.

Father LaFarge often thought that a plain wooden chair would have served him better. Or perhaps he might even have the casters fixed. He had decided, though, to keep things as they were. This would help to remind him that thrones can tumble.

His desk was piled high with letters, mostly from well-wishers congratulating him on his promotion.

146

There were some letter-writers, though, that did not mention his ability. Their letters implied that he would now be too busy to "meddle in matters outside of his field."

For instance, there was the letter he had received in the mail that morning from the gentleman who, not many months before, had threatened to report him to the Cardinal. Father LaFarge took this letter from the top of the pile and reread it thoughtfully.

> *Dear Father LaFarge [the letter began]:*
>
> *I was happy to hear that you have been appointed editor-in-chief of* America. *Though I rarely agree with statements made by your magazine, I have to admit that you try to be fair by offering more than one point of view.*
>
> *I regret the unpleasantness at our past encounter, but still hold no brief for priests meddling in matters outside the Church. You will probably have your hands full now and stick to your writing. To me, this seems better than chasing lost causes.*

He put the letter down. It was typical of many he had received. Father LaFarge could not accept an attitude that put such limits on the role of priests. Surely it was the duty of every clergyman to work toward brotherhood. It was not enough to preach from the pulpit.

Father LaFarge glanced down at a pad on which he had listed his many duties for the day. One item was underlined in red pencil: an appointment at three o'clock with the Father Provincial, who was his old friend and superior, Father Kelly. Father LaFarge looked up at his clock: its hands pointed to one-thirty. Suddenly, then, he realized that the clock was not ticking. He had forgotten to wind the clock again! From now on, he had better leave this chore to one of the several members of the staff who had offered to take it on. Father Kelly would probably pop in at any moment. At this thought, he abruptly began to settle his desk, causing two of the casters to come off.

Of course, when the Father Provincial entered, he found the editor-in-chief crawling on all fours.

"I still can't understand why you don't have those casters fixed, John," he said. "But I suppose you have your special reason."

When he had inserted the casters in the chair, Father LaFarge struggled to his feet and offered his superior the honored seat. "But I warn you," he added, "you'll be safer on one of the others."

"I'd prefer that," Father Kelly said drily. "Living dangerously is for poets and dreamers."

The two friends then spoke briefly of the past, and of those days on the Ridge when Father Kelly had warned his assistant pastor not to move too fast.

"I believe I told you, John, that one cannot work wonders over-night," he now said. "But in your case, I was probably wrong. You've accomplished a great deal in a short time."

Father LaFarge chuckled and said, "Many people still think I'm in too much of a hurry. As a matter of fact, there are those who disapprove of everything I do."

"I know," Father Kelly said. "How well I know." Scarcely a week went by without some sort of complaint concerning Father LaFarge's work in race relations. Even some members of his own order were critical.

"But I didn't come to talk about those who disagree with you, John," the Father Provincial went on, "but to say how pleased I am about your appointment."

They talked for a while, and then Father Kelly glanced up at the clock.

"I have an important meeting at four, but I see there's still plenty of time," he said.

Panicking briefly, Father LaFarge put in, "I'm sorry, but it's stopped."

"Stopped—?"

"Yes, the clock, I mean."

Father Kelly shook his head, as one might at a naughty child.

"Well, in that case I'd best be off. First, though, I'd like to give you a bit of advice. Assign one of your assistants to wind the clock. And do be careful, John, not to let the wrong kind of people use you for their own ends."

Father Provincial tried to put on a long face, but it didn't work. He could not hide a smile as the two old friends shook hands.

The rest of the day was as hectic as all the others. Father LaFarge had a meeting with the staff, rewrote an editorial, called the printer to inquire about galley proofs overdue, and answered a stack of mail. As he was dictating a final letter into his recording machine for the faithful secretary-librarian, William H. Dodd, to transcribe, a young novice priest—whose gift for writing poetry had brought him to *America*—came into the office and announced that Father LaFarge had a visitor.

The timid young poet flushed and said, "I tried to tell him it was after hours, but he seemed most anxious to see you."

"After hours?"

The editor glanced up at the clock, which still had not been wound. "What time is it?" he asked, "and who is my guest?"

He was told it was six o'clock, and the visitor was Mr. A. Philip Randolph.

"Show Mr. Randolph in, please," Father LaFarge said. "I'll be on the terrace. I'd like some light refreshments served, too, if it isn't too much trouble."

When the novice turned and started to leave the room, Father LaFarge added, "Will you please see that clock is wound every day. From now on, this will be one of your daily chores."

The young man couldn't have looked more pleased if he had been ordered to write a column.

On their rooftop terrace Father LaFarge and Mr. Randolph talked. They had often met at interracial gatherings. Father LaFarge's visitor was President of the Brotherhood of Sleeping Car Porters, and one of the few Negroes who had risen to importance in the labor movement. The reason for his visit, Mr. Randolph said, was to interest the priest in a rally that was to be held in Madison Square Garden a few weeks later. There was need for a demonstration at this time, Mr. Randolph said, to protest against unfair employment practices. He pointed out that it was difficult for

Negroes to get decent jobs, even though labor was scarce during wartime.

"You know I have deep concern for the Negro," Father LaFarge said. He was about to accept the invitation, when he remembered Father Kelly's words: "Be careful, John, not to let the wrong kind of people use you for their own ends."

"I must speak bluntly," he said. "If the rally is being backed by radicals, I must decline."

Mr. Randolph assured him that this was not the case. He had no illusions about those who pretended to be interested in his people's welfare. They were the ones who had wanted only to spread discontent among the Negroes, or to create doubts concerning democracy.

"As a matter of fact," Mr. Randolph went on, "I received a check for $25,000 from the Communist Party to help defray the expenses for the rally. I promptly returned it."

"That was a brave thing to do," Father LaFarge said.

"Not at all," Mr. Randolph replied. "Most of my people have no use for Nazis, Fascists, or their work. They are deeply American, believe in democracy, and are willing to fight for it, at home and abroad."

But, he went on to warn, their love of country could change. No one enjoyed being a second-class citizen. Injustices had to be corrected. Twisted ideas thrived on misery.

Father LaFarge agreed completely. This was a view that he had always held; indeed, it was the watchword of *America*.

"And, if you so wish, Mr. Randolph," he said "I shall be honored to speak at your rally."

Father LaFarge gazed out at the sea of faces—the largest gathering he had ever addressed. The spirit here was truly American and bound by no ties to any foreign land.

He was the only white man on the platform. He spoke, as had all the others, on equality and justice. These were commands handed down by Christ, Father LaFarge said.

When he took his seat again, he noticed that too few of the clergy were present. He thanked God for having given him the grace to speak out against injustice, and he prayed that more of his fellow priests would join the fight.

His appearance at the rally was followed by much abusive mail. Father LaFarge did not care. That historic meeting had the desired result. Soon afterward, President Franklin D. Roosevelt issued a new order on fair employment practices.

It was the Lenten season in 1947. Father LaFarge had been ordered to stay in bed. Recently he had been told he would have to undergo a serious operation—the third in a few years—and he had been given orders to rest. As a matter of fact, so many of his fellow Jesuits were keeping an eye on him that he often pretended to sleep. But he could not now, nor did he want to. Father LaFarge decided to get dressed.

It was quite early in the morning, and he thought that by walking quietly he could get to his office without being discovered. Not certain just why he wanted to go there, he tiptoed down the corridor. Once inside the familiar room, it became clear why he had wished to come. He yearned to be reassured that he had done his job well. And this, he realized, was unusual. Indeed, he feared that this need for reassurance was a form of pride. Still, it would be comforting to know that current business was completed and in order. If this was pride he would surely be forgiven.

From a worn folder he took out a sheet of paper that summarized the policy of *America* since he had been editor-in-chief. If he were to die during the operation, it was important to think about the past now. In this way he could match his aims against what had been accomplished. He moved toward the desk, paper in hand, and gingerly sat down. Head lowered, he gazed at the sheet and read:

(1) *Our Duties Toward the International Community and Its Organization*

(2) *Our Obligation of Charity Toward the War-Stricken People of the World*

(3) *The Issue of Morality in the Market Place and the Consequent Reform of Certain Economic Institutions*

(4) *The Question of Civil Rights and Minority Groups—Whether Religious or Racial Minorities*

These issues had been the chief concern of *America*, as they still were. Sadly, Father LaFarge thought, few of the problems had been solved. Mankind was more sharply divided than before. Instead of brotherhood, the world was still torn apart with fear and suspicion. Instead of achieving peace, the United Nations was often being used to increase hostilities. The rich were still protesting against reforms so sorely needed by the poor. The horrors that resulted from Hitler's racist ideas had not taught man the folly of thinking oneself better . . .

The sun was high in the sky by now, and Spring was in the air. Suddenly, Father LaFarge felt that he must go out. He put the papers in the folder and stood up. The motion caused a caster to come off. There was a crash; now his prowling would be discovered.

Almost at once, a voice in the corridor cried out, "Who's in there?"

"Me," Father LaFarge replied, then amended, "or, if I want to be grammatical, I should say 'It is I.' "

He heard the door open and a voice said, "But—but where are you?"

"Down here, on a treasure hunt as usual."

In pained tones the other said, "Oh, do get up, Father, let *me!*"

The voice was that of a young member of the staff. He was leaning down to help his superior rise.

"Thank you, I can get up myself," Father LaFarge said. "I know I'm old, but I'm not that old."

The young man protested. Father LaFarge was actually very young. Indeed, he was as alert and active of mind as anyone in Campion House. While voicing his admiration, the young colleague found the caster and put it in its place.

"When I heard the noise," he said, "I thought it might be a prowler."

"Thieves are too smart for that," Father LaFarge

replied. "Anyone who tried to steal from Jesuits would be running the risk of having us beg from them."

The young man laughed, and then reminded his superior that he was supposed to rest.

"I've tried to sleep," Father LaFarge said, "but it's impossible. As a matter of fact, I've decided to go out."

"But you're not supposed to walk."

He didn't intend to walk, Father LaFarge put in. And to prove it he said, "Would you please order a cab for me?"

The young man did not move. He seemed about to argue.

"If you don't call a cab, I'll do so myself," Father LaFarge said. "Furthermore, I'm sure I can trust you not to speak of this."

This was perhaps the young man's most difficult decision concerning the rule of obedience. He looked deeply worried, but finally he said, "I will do what you ask, Father."

"No need to look so forlorn," his superior said. "I'm feeling very fit."

By what seemed a small miracle, he managed to leave the building alone just as the cab pulled up.

The driver regarded his fare with suspicion, and asked "Where to, Reverend?"

"First," Father LaFarge told him, "I'd like to have a look at the Statue of Liberty."

This would be quite expensive, he was told.

"How much?"

"Oh . . . about six bucks."

He had only three.

"We'll skip that," the priest said. "How much to Harlem?"

"You should be ashamed," Father LaFarge said.
"This is a holy man."

"About four, both ways—if you want me to wait. Do you want to come back?"

"No."

"Any special place in Harlem?" the driver asked, in a way that suggested that his passenger might be crazy.

"There's a church," Father LaFarge explained. He wasn't sure about the street, exactly, but maybe if they'd drive around a bit, he'd recognize it.

Meanwhile, the meter was ticking merrily on. It had

reached $2.60 and he wanted to give the man a tip.

"I'll get out here," he said. He paid the puzzled driver and started to walk. It didn't really matter which church, as long as they sang spirituals. As a matter of fact, the section was dotted with churches. He ducked into one. He sat in the rear pew for a while, listening as the congregation swayed and sang. The strains of "Let My People Go" sounded a mournful plea. Curiously, the priest's heart lightened. Yes, he had truly tried. . . .

He decided to leave before the services were over, not wishing to call attention to himself, but he was stopped by one of the deacons at the door.

"Aren't you Reverend LaFarge?" the man asked.

"I am" he said, smiling.

"You are most welcome, any time," the deacon said. "Thank you for coming, Reverend."

Outside, he was reminded of the Ridge—especially the little girls in their white starched cotton dresses. Father LaFarge walked on, past tenements so over-crowded that people seemed to have spilled out on the streets. The city had been no Promised Land for these people.

Before long, he turned a corner and abruptly found himself in front of a Jewish synagogue. This year Easter and Passover happened to come together, and

Father LaFarge found this quite fitting. He recalled the words of Christ: "I did not come to destroy the law, but to fulfill it."

He was sharply recalled from his reverie by the sound of shouting voices. On the steps of the small synagogue he saw an old man wearing a prayer shawl and yarmulka. Below on the sidewalk, a group of boys were calling him names.

Father LaFarge shoved through the circle of tormentors, and, without raising his voice, said, "You should be ashamed. This is a holy man—a priest of God."

At the sight of the tall priest and the anger in his eyes, the gang melted away.

After drawing himself up to his full height, the man on the steps said, "I would rather be called 'Rabbi.'"

The priest smiled and answered, "*Pax Vobiscum,* Rabbi."

"*Shalom,* friend," the rabbi replied.

Somehow the world seemed bright again. He had, indeed, tried, Father LaFarge thought. And no more was required of him than to serve God in an ordinary way.

A cab pulled up to the curb and an Irish voice sang out. "Merciful heaven, what are you doing so far from home, Father?"

The priest wasn't even sure where the two of them had met. But the driver knew him, obviously, and when he added, "Hop in, and I'll take you back to Campion House," Father LaFarge hopped in.

He would have to borrow the fare from his future allowance. It didn't matter, though; his journey had been worth it.

10

God Had Chosen

EVEN AFTER their editor-in-chief was up and about again, everyone around Campion House tried to protect him. "Father shouldn't do this and he shouldn't do that," they all said. Besides, Father Provincial had given strict orders that he "must not try to move too fast." Father LaFarge knew that all this stemmed from their worry about his health. He had been quite seriously ill. But, as he put it, God had guided the hand of Dr. William MacFee, who had taken him apart and put him together again. This time, miraculously, to stay put.

So he would look at those who were trying to hold him back and say, "Only the good die young." And he was a mere 65—just starting out!

Evidently the news of his illness had been spread around, and he had been amazed—positively amazed—at the many gifts and letters and messages from friends who wished him well. Now, when he went for a short walk, people stopped him on the way to tell him they were glad to see him hale and hearty again. Usually another Jesuit went along. Father La-Farge obviously was not to be trusted to take care of himself. Indeed, so many watchful eyes were on him, he couldn't help wondering if word had leaked out about his adventure in Harlem. He asked the young assistant about this one day when they were out for a stroll.

The answer was No. His confidence had not been betrayed.

As they moved along, they were greeted from all sides, especially by the children. Their high-pitched "Hiya, Father LaFarge," was sweet music to the priest.

His young companion said, "You should be called 'the Pied Piper Priest.' "

Father LaFarge smiled.

The sidewalks of New York now were little different from the dirt roads of the Ridge.

Before long, he took up his work again as editor-in-chief. While he was in the hospital, two things in his office had been changed. The old clock now made no sound. An electric one stood in its place. And the casters no longer came off his chair. When he had asked why these things had been altered during his absence, he was told that the Father Provincial had ordered it so. This had been confirmed the next time the two met.

"You're not as limber as you used to be, John," Father Kelly had told him. "You've got too much work to do to risk taking a spill."

Although he felt no less limber than before, Father LaFarge hadn't argued. He did have much work to do.

Nowadays he was often asked to give talks at gatherings of non-Catholics. Father LaFarge always welcomed this. To understand the beliefs of others was surely a step toward brotherhood. He was also very happy to be invited to deliver the "Dudleian" Lecture at the School of Divinity of Harvard University. In the years when he had been a student there, this would have been impossible for a Catholic priest.

He spoke to a large audience at his alma mater, and summed up his present philosophy.

"The sorry state of the world," he said, "suggests that many former concepts about man must be considered obsolete in the light of all that has happened."

He stressed that one human right could not be chosen in preference to another, nor could human rights be asserted only for certain groups, while other groups were excluded. "For unless the whole of man speaks for the whole of *mankind*," he insisted, "the statement has no meaning."

The tone of his speech seemed to cause surprise in some quarters. Later, in a group discussion, one of the faculty members said, "You make it sound as if the Vatican is catching up with modern times. Or do you just wish it were so?"

Father LaFarge assured the man that all he had said was compatible with the Church's teachings. In fact, he continued, he had recently received a letter from Pope Pius XII. The Holy Father had pointed out that extreme nationalism closed its eyes to the needs of the human family—that racial injustice was a sin against one's brother, and that economic selfishness could not be condoned.

"That's interesting," the Protestant faculty member said. "But do you feel such ideas are put into practice in the Church?"

Father LaFarge agreed that many Catholics—even members of the clergy—were not fully aware of the Church's teaching. Indeed, even when they were, they did not always follow it. "True charity is very rare," he said. "Isn't this so among members of your faith too?"

"Yes," the other replied. "But the Roman Catholic Church still seems more backward in many respects. Take race relations, for instance. By the way, Father, how long have you been interested in the Negro cause?"

"About thirty-eight years," the priest said, "since I worked on the Ridge."

"Amazing!"

When Father LaFarge was fully recovered, it was decided that he should again go to Europe. From there he could give a first-hand report to his readers on postwar conditions overseas.

While in Rome he decided to call on his cousin Lena, a niece of his father's who was now the Marchesa Morelli di Stellara. He had been anxious about her ever since he had read that the street she lived on had been practically wiped out by a bomb. His cousin, though, proved very much alive. As the aged Marchesa put it, "The good Lord protected me. I had nothing damaged but a plate-glass door."

This, she went on to say, was probably because in spite of being old and stone-deaf, she had still had enough sense not to believe the Fascist propaganda. She was young at heart, Cousin Lena boasted, and still able to adapt to modern ideas. The proof of this was her attitude toward Ascenzio, her devoted cook for almost thirty years. He was now out on strike.

"Still," she went on tolerantly, "how can the dear old man resist the spirit of the age?"

This seemed almost a revolutionary statement, coming from a descendant of *Bonne Maman!*

While in Rome he had a private audience with the Pope. The Holy Father's friendly and informal manner at once put him at ease. They spoke on many subjects but Father LaFarge was especially eager to hear the

Pope's views about bridging the barriers between Catholics and people of other faiths.

Instead of answering, the Holy Father suggested that his visitor state his own opinions on the subject. Eagerly Father LaFarge told of his belief that discussions about differences was one of the ways to combat false ideas.

"Surely," he said, "such an exchange between men of good will might help overcome the damage done by bigots."

The Holy Father smiled and said, "Work out these ideas in more detail and send them to me."

After a few days with his friends at the Jesuit headquarters close by the Vatican, Father LaFarge left for Paris. From France he was flown by an Army plane to Strasbourg, and finally he went by car into Germany. He was amazed at the informal way a guard allowed the car to pass from Alsace into Baden. How splendid it would be, the priest thought, if someday all artificial barriers between nations could be replaced by trust. Though such hope must lie in the distant future, he was heartened by small signs of reconciliation.

At Offenberg he visited a newly-established cultural center, where German and French students met for the first time since the war. On a train to Frankfurt,

German passengers no longer turned away in fear. He took part in a discussion about the recent arrival of a carload of potatoes from Austria. Old wounds were being healed by the gift of food.

The subject turned from potatoes to orchestras and their leaders. Father LaFarge joined in with stories about the New York Philharmonic and the Boston Symphony. Before long, melodious strains were being hummed, and later, when talk turned to a comparison of musicians from both countries, it was without heat or rivalry.

Father decided he could not leave Germany without making a trip to Coblenz to see his old friend Dr. Chardon. The streets of Coblenz were piled high with rubble, with pathways through it much like the narrow paths between New England snowdrifts. When he arrived at what had once been Dr. Chardon's church, there was nothing left but a few walls and a basement, which was now occupied by the pastor's assistant. The courtyard was filled with youngsters who were gaily carrying away the rubble in wheelbarrows. How different they looked from the marching puppets he had seen on his previous visit!

After his first greeting, Dr. Chardon pointed to a void above one of the walls and said, "That's where we talked the last time you were here."

*The courtyard was filled with youngsters
carrying away the rubble in wheelbarrows.*

The two had much to talk about. Father LaFarge learned of many friends and acquaintances who had died in Nazi prisons—some merely because they refused to close their churches, and others for speaking out against Hitler.

On all sides Father LaFarge saw misery and destruction. But now the countries that had leveled the land were doing all they could to bring peace and order in the midst of ruin.

The waste of war weighed heavily upon him. Surely, he thought, now that they had perfected a bomb that could destroy all mankind, a new beginning must be made toward brotherhood.

Before returning to America, the traveling editor stopped again in Paris. There, at a press conference, he heard of the Marshall Plan. This American program to aid with food and materials for war-torn Europe warmed his heart. His countrymen were generous. They did not care for war; they had no wish to conquer. And now these suffering people, friend and enemy alike, would be housed and clothed and fed.

By the time Father LaFarge arrived at Shannon Airport in Ireland, he was in high spirits. From here he would take a plane to America. At the airport, luncheon and beer were being served. This was the first real beer he had seen on the entire trip. Even in Munich, famed for its beer in pre-war days, the beer had been a dark and bitter brew.

A neatly-dressed waiter moved to the priest and asked:

"Would Your Reverence like a glass of beer?"

"And sure," he said, "I would."

"And it will be 25¢," the waiter said.

"But I have no 25¢," the priest replied. "I have no American money with me."

"Then it will be a shilling, Your Reverence," the waiter said.

With a jolt, Father LaFarge remembered that his only bit of English money was locked up in his bag on the plane.

"Then you have no money at all?" the waiter asked.

"That's exactly the problem."

"Well," the waiter said, "in that case, the only thing is for the Government of Ireland to provide you with the beer. We want to make everybody who passes through Shannon Airport joyful and contented."

Somewhat later, a newspaper reporter approached Father LaFarge and said, "May I ask where Your Reverence has been traveling? I understand you have been moving about quite a bit."

The priest said this was so. He had been in Rome and Paris and Germany.

"And did you see the Pope?" the reporter asked.

"Certainly I saw the Pope."

The reporter's eyes twinkled when he said, "And I understand also that you had a glass of beer at the expense of our Government."

Then the man added that this was a matter of historical record. Such details were of interest to the general public.

By now, Father LaFarge felt as though he had drunk a gallon of beer.

A few days later, in New York, he met Tom Doyle, a reporter for the Religious News Service, which prepares news stories about religious events for papers and publications throughout the nation. Mr. Doyle looked even more mischievous than usual.

"Did you enjoy your trip, Father?" he asked.

"I had a wonderful time," Father LaFarge replied. "I saw everybody from the Pope down."

"It was nice to know," Doyle went on, "that the Irish Government treated you to a glass of beer. It appeared in a Dublin paper and they wired it over here."

This seemed much ado about a small thing, Father LaFarge replied. And he hoped—he truly did—that Tom Doyle would not use this item in his column.

He wouldn't, Tom promised, but then added that Father LaFarge was always "news." The priest thanked his fellow reporter. Should the word get about that he had locked up his money in his suitcase, he would be in for plenty of free "advice."

Not long after his return from Europe, Father La-Farge was informed that the duties of editor-in-chief were now too strenuous for him, and that he would have to take an easier job. He would, of course, remain on the staff of his magazine as an editorial associate. This would give him more time to write books and work in civic causes.

Three years later, in 1951, he was asked by the State Department to spend several weeks in Germany as a visiting consultant. His superiors encouraged him to go. They were interested to learn about the activities of various religious groups in a reviving Europe.

For the most part, what Father LaFarge now saw gave him hope for the future. Ruins were giving way to new apartments; cities hummed with activity. Religious groups were playing a large part in reconstruction, and churches were crowded as they had been before. Indeed, Father LaFarge thought, it sometimes seemed that there had been no war.

Then he spent a few days in Berlin. He stayed at a beautiful suburb that had not been damaged in the war. In a large lovely villa, with a porch and garden and cherry blossoms, it almost seemed as though he were back in Newport. But this impression did not last long. Day and night, refugees drifted into the villa, after they had crossed from the Russian zone of Berlin. This city divided in two reminded him of the many countries now held by Communists. Those people beyond the Iron Curtain were not free to speak or write. But, saddest of all, they had to pray in secret.

11

Love Unlimited

IN 1952 FATHER LAFARGE learned that a group of
friends had been conspiring to give a dinner in his
honor. It was to be held at the Waldorf-Astoria in
commemoration of his twenty-five years on the staff of
America. At first it was planned to be a quite modest
affair, including only his closest friends, but when the
news got out that he was to be honored, there was a
stampede of people who wanted to attend. A great
variety of people considered themselves "close
friends." Thus, the affair had swelled to a few hundred. When he heard about this, Father LaFarge said,
"Why should a few more or less matter?"

He expected that someone would again comment on
his wide but not always too wise fellowship. What if
they did? A few more or less did *not* matter.

The day before the dinner, a visitor was announced.
The priest who brought the message reported that it
didn't seem to be anyone important—just a young
"colored" man.

176

To Father LaFarge, it seemed confused thinking to judge a person by his looks, and he told his young assistant so. He especially disliked the idea of mentioning color. Was his guest perhaps green or maybe purple?

The messenger stammered, "But, Father, I didn't mean—"

Again, Father LaFarge interrupted. "Furthermore," he said, "you should be careful not to judge people on the basis of their age. A great deal can be learned by listening to the young."

This was as close to scolding as he ever came, and the young priest now looked deeply distressed. Although he had not raised his voice, Father LaFarge felt guilty. He would have to apologize for his outburst.

When he reached the small reception room, he spied a young man gazing out of the window. He was tall and lean, and held his head high in an attitude of defiance.

"You wanted to see me?" Father LaFarge asked.

His visitor wheeled about. The priest caught his breath in astonishment. This lad was so like Jeb Jenks that it seemed he could be no other. "Sit down, please," the priest said.

"I'm not staying long," he said. "I'm not even sure why I came."

"Well, now that you did, why not rest a while?"

Almost grudgingly, his guest seated himself across from Father LaFarge. Then, instead of explaining the reason for his visit, he silently examined his host. Finally, his story came rushing out in a stream of words. He just happened to be in New York visiting some relatives of his mother. He had read in the paper about a dinner being given for Father LaFarge. The name was familiar to him.

"Well, anyhow, I got curious, and that's why I'm here," he concluded.

"Who told you about me?" the priest asked.

"My father. Seems I was christened after you. My name's John Jenks."

Jeb's son! He should have known, of course.

"And how is your father, John?"

"He's pretty good."

He supposed the priest knew that his family lived in Baltimore. It was not too bad a place, as cities go, he said. He, though, preferred it further North. But even here, equal opportunity for Negroes was a sham.

He was an angry young man and Father LaFarge knew the many reasons why. Still, he wanted Jeb's son to do the talking. After a brooding silence John Jenks did precisely that.

"Take my own father, for instance," he went on.

"You can't find a better mechanic than my father. True, he had a fairly decent job before he went into the Service, but what has he done since then? Dirty work around garages—that's what he's done. Once in a while, they let him tinker with a screw or nut, but it was mostly dirty work. Where can a man get a job without belonging to a union? And most unions kept the Negroes out. Do you know that, Father?"

"I do," the priest told John. "I know of all these many injustices. Is your father as bitter as you?"

"No," said the son. "My folks go to church."

After a stony silence, the boy announced that he didn't care much for the clergy. Especially the white clergy. It was high time they told people to practice what they preached.

"My father said you always did," he added. "But I'm not sure."

Father LaFarge remembered young Jeb and his charcoal, blackening the hands and face of Christ in the picture book. What his son was feeling now was much the same. But this lad was older, had hoped and suffered longer. What could he say?

Father LaFarge spoke of his days on the Ridge, of how he and Jeb had been the closest of friends. He went on to tell his guest that there were many white clergymen deeply committed to the interracial cause.

True, some had remained silent for too long, but this certainly would be corrected.

"*When?*" John Jenks cried out. "All the white man says is 'wait.' "

"I know, John," Father LaFarge told his namesake, "but the wrong kind of speed will only bring suffering to your people."

"I'm not sure of that," John said, "I need more time to think it over."

As he left, though, he seemed less angry, and the priest said he hoped John would visit him again.

"Maybe," John said. "I need time to think that over, too."

Nonetheless, he didn't refuse a handshake—and that was a good sign.

At the anniversary dinner, Father LaFarge told the audience that he had once been called "a champion of lost causes." If he had ever believed this was true, he could not now as he gazed at the faces of his many friends.

People of every faith were there, and some of no faith at all.

After his speech, the priest was presented with a chalice, the work of a gifted silversmith, Louis Feron. In trembling tones he told his friends that they would be in his prayers whenever he raised this chalice at Mass. In this way, he said, their beautiful and generous gift would become part of the never-ending renewal of God's love.

As the priest and his party were leaving the hotel, there seemed to be some sort of argument going on outside the door.

The bell captain was saying sharply, "I told you three times now to stand aside, boy. You'd better move."

The answer came, "I'm no 'boy' and I'm not going to move."

Father LaFarge stood gazing at an angry-faced John Jenks.

"Didn't have money for the dinner," Jeb's son mumbled, "but I wanted to say congratulations."

Father LaFarge beamed. He spread his arms and proudly said, "Gentlemen, meet my namesake. This is John Jenks."

Late in the summer of 1962, Father LaFarge made a final visit to his old home in Newport. The last members of his Newport family had either died or moved away. Soon all the furnishings would be parceled out and distributed among the heirs and family friends. A Jesuit of eighty-two should have no yearning for these

Father LaFarge spread his arms and said,
"Gentlemen, meet my namesake."

things, he thought. Yet, they seemed to hold some message for him.

The air was chill; so he gathered up some old newspapers and a few sticks from the old wood closet. His fingers did not have to fumble for the silver box on the gray stone mantel. He drew out a match and started a small fire in the library fireplace, then sat in an easy chair for a few moments and let his thoughts wander back over the years.

The flames flickered as they had done during those days and nights of his boyhood. Small mementos were in every corner of the big old frame house. Nobody else left now to remember them. He gazed toward the place where his brothers had hung their fishing tackle, the triangular closet for carpenter's tools, the drawers in the library bookcase for old letters and photographs.

Each item in the house brought back memories. The bookshelves reminded him of school and college and visits to the library; prayerbooks recalled the parish church and his early friends. Here he had grown up in an atmosphere of confidence, of love and faith and friendship.

"Let not the pains and joys of belonging to a family ever be taken from our land," he prayed.

After a quiet, timeless reverie, he went upstairs, and

into his old room. There was no longer need to gaze through isinglass panes in the nursery stove, as into a crystal ball. He had become what God had chosen him to be.

Father LaFarge died at the age of eighty-three, on November 24, 1963. He died peacefully in the night. On the next morning, he was discovered with a sheet of newspaper characteristically clutched in his hand. His epitaph might have been words he himself had written:

"Nothing will convert the world short of a gospel of limitless love . . . faithfulness to the rights of the humblest person, and to our pledges with man and God."

INDEX

Adams, Henry, 12 f., 17, 45, 56–59
Adams, John, President, 57
Adams, John Quincy, President, 57
America, periodical, 126, 128 f., 138, 146, 154 f., 176
Ascension Church, New York, 18, 102

Bartholdi, Frederick August, sculptor, 46 f.
Beale, Mrs. Jennie, 121–124
Benes, Eduard, president of Czechoslovakia, 137
Berlin, Germany, 136 f., 174 f.
Blackwells Island, New York, 105–107
Brenton, Jahleel, 38
Brenton's Reef, R. I., 21, 38, 41
Budapest, Hungary, 132, 135

Callahan, Daniel, S.J., 93–100, 104
Cambridge, Mass., 64, 67, 70–76. *See also* Harvard University
Campion House, New York, 128, 146, 156, 162, 163

Cardinal Gibbons Institute, 125, 129, 140
Casey, John, S.J., 105
Catholic Interracial Council, 138 f. *See also* Hunton, George K.
Chardon, Heinrich, 79, 89, 133–135, 169
Chartres cathedral, 59
Christitch, Annie O'Brien, 132
Coblenz, Germany, 134 f., 169–171
Coddington Public School, Newport, 29
Columbia University, 64
Communism (Marxism), 80, 120, 175
Copeland, Charles, professor, 71
Cronan, Philip, Reverend, 21, 65

Dodd, William H., 150
Doyle, Tom, 173

Emerick, Abraham J., S.J., 116
Eucharistic Congress, Budapest, 132, 135

185

Fairchild, Neil, 35, 67 f.
Fascism, 132–136, 167
Franklin, Benjamin, 27

Gibbons, James, Cardinal. *See* Cardinal Gibbons Institute

Haile Selassie, Emperor, 135 f.
Harlem, New York City, 159
Harvard College (University), 61, 64, 67–76, 99
Harvard Divinity School, 73, 165
Hill, Perry, 12, 16, 37
Hill, Catherine, 12, 16, 62
Hill, Walter, 12, 14, 16, 29, 37, 55, 62
Hill's (Mrs.) School, 12 ff., 21, 29
Hitler, Adolf, 132 f., 135, 137. *See also* Nazism
Hooper, Mabel, 76
Hudson River State Mental Hospital, 96
Hughes, Rufus, 118
Hunton, George K., 125, 138–145. *See also* Catholic Interracial Council

Innsbruck, University of, 76–91, 99
Interracial Justice (book), 136
Ireland, 171–173
Irwin, Agnes, Radcliffe College dean, 70

James, Henry, 60, 83–88
James, William, 60, 61, 73 f.
Jenkintown, Pa., 25
Jesuits. *See* Society of Jesus
Johnson, Henry, 118
Jones, Mrs. Mary ("Aunt Pigeon"), 111–113, 124

Kakuzo, Okakura, 22–25
Kelly, Laurence, S.J., 108–111, 128, 148–150, 165
Kohut, Mr., 118 f.

LaFarge, Bancel, brother, 11, 16 f., 19, 33, 39–42, 63, 76, 90
LaFarge, Emily, sister, 11, 20, 34, 44 f., 63
LaFarge, Frances, sister, 11, 15, 18 f., 57, 65
LaFarge, Grant, brother, 15, 19, 63, 65–67, 76 f.
LaFarge, Mrs. Jean Frédéric de ("Bonne Maman"), grandmother, 34, 52–54
LaFarge, John, S.J.: appointed *America* editor, 146; appointed *America* staff, 128 f.; and Cardinal Gibbons Institute, 125, 129; and Catholic Interracial Council, 138 and *passim;* death, 184; education (preparatory), 11 ff., 29, 61, 64; enters Jesuits, 91; in Europe, 132–137; 167–171; 174 f.; family background, 11–13, 22,

26–28, 32, 36, 42 f., 52–54, 72 f.; first Communion, 43; first Mass, 90; first sermon, 96; Harvard studies, 67–76; health, 56, 61, 64, 71, 83, 99 f., 102–104, 154, 163 f.; hospital chaplain, 96; interracial and brotherhood work, 110–116, 117, 119, 121, 138–145, 149, 151–154, 165 f., 168 f., 171, 177–181; in Ireland, 171–173; and Msgr. Ligutti, 131; linguistic talent, 52 f., 54, 81; musical talent, 53, 75; novitiate, 93–97; ordination, 90; parish work, 105, 108–128; penmanship, 32 f., 35–37, 72, 94; Phi Beta Kappa award, 75; prison chaplain, 105–107; reception as Jesuit, 97; seminary studies, 76–91; teaching, 97; at Vatican, 136, 166–168, 173; vocation to priesthood, 59, 65 f., 76 f., 89 f.; Woodstock studies, 97–104

LaFarge, John, father, 44–46, 48–53, 56–59, 100–103

LaFarge, Margaret, mother, 11–64, 83–88, 90, 127 f.

LaFarge, Margaret, sister, 11, 15, 41 f., 83, 90, 127 f.

LaFarge, Oliver, brother, 12, 15, 18, 34, 64, 125

LaFarge, Raymond, brother, 19

LaFayette, Marie-Jean-Paul, Marquise de, 54

Lennon, John, 107

Liberty, Statue of, 46 f.

Ligutti, Luigi, Monsignor, 131

Loyola College (Baltimore), 97

S.S. *Lusitania*, 121

MacFee, William F., M.D., 163

McKinley, William, President, 81

Marshall Plan, 171

Maryland (Southern). *See* The Ridge; St. Aloysius Parish; St. George's Island; St. Inigoes; St. James Church; St. Thomas Manor

Marxism. *See* Communism

Masaryk, Jan, 132 f.

Matthews, James Brent, S.J., 116

Morelli di Stellara, Lena, Marchesa, 167

Morton, Levi P., U. S. Minister to France, 46

Mussolini, Benito, 135 f.

National Association for the Advancement of the Colored People (NAACP), 140 f.

National Catholic Rural Life Conference, 131

Nazism, 132–137; 169–171

New York City, N. Y., 51, 61, 62, 63, 64, 105 f., 129 f.

Newport, R. I., 11, 14, 18, 38, 43, 60, 67 f., 70, 71, 89, 127, 128, 175, 181

Parsons, Wilfred, S.J., 128

Pearl Harbor, Hawaii, 137

Pepper, William, 42

Perry, Mrs. Christopher Grant ("Nonna"), grandmother, 26–28, 42 f., 53, 113

Perry, Thomas Sergeant, uncle, 22, 75

Perry, Matthew Calbraith, Commodore, 27 f.

Perry, Oliver Hazard, Commodore, 27

Philadelphia, Pa., 25 f., 42 f., 105

Pius XI, Pope, 136

Pius XII, Pope, 166–168, 173

Portrait of a Lady, novel by Henry James, 60

Radcliffe College, 69, 70

Randolph, A. Philip, 151–153

Redwood Library, Newport, 39, 48, 54 f.

"The Ridge," 108–129, 160, 166

Rogers High School, Newport, 61

Rome, Italy, 135 f., 167 f.

Roosevelt, Franklin D., President, 154

Roosevelt, Theodore, President, 66 f., 77, 81

Sacred Heart, Religious of the, 43

St. Aloysius Parish, Leonardtown, Md., 108–111

St. George's Island, Maryland, 120

St. Inigoes, Maryland, 110, 111–128, *passim*

St. James Church, St. Inigoes, Md., 117

St. Joseph's Church, Philadelphia, 105

St. Mary's Church, Newport, 38, 76, 128

St. Paul's Church, Cambridge, Mass., 74 f.

St. Thomas Manor, Maryland, 104

Sergeant, Thomas, Judge, 26

Sisson, Mr., 33, 35 f.

Sleeping Car Porters, Brotherhood of, 151

Smith, William, 33, 39–43

Society of Jesus (Jesuits), 78, 81. 82, 83, 90 f., 93, 97, 99, and *passim*

The Sunlight, magazine, 37 f.

Talbot, Francis X., S.J., 130 f.

Vatican, 136, 166–168

Warren, Schuyler N., 125

Wharton, Edith, author, 14

Wilson, Woodrow, President, 121

Woodstock College, 97–104, *passim*

Woolsey, Sarah, author, 14

About the Author

FLORA STROUSSE is a native of Baltimore, Maryland, and attended Maryland Institute in that city. After her marriage she moved to Philadelphia, where she has since resided. While her children were young she worked in various social fields and later engaged in editorial work with various publishing firms.

Mrs. Strousse has studied English and creative writing at Temple University, the University of Pennsylvania, and the Bread Loaf Writers Conference. Her short stories have appeared in many magazines, and one of them was included in the collection *All Manner of Men*, edited by Riley Hughes. Her books for young and adult readers include *The Friar and the Knight, Margaret Haughery*, and *John Fitzgerald Kennedy* (all written for the American Background Books series), *John Milton*, and *The Littlest Christmas Tree*. The story of President Kennedy was reprinted in paperback by New American Library.

AMERICAN BACKGROUND BOOKS

Lives of Catholic Heroes and Heroines
in American History

AMERICAN BACKGROUND BOOKS are stories for boys and girls from eight to fourteen and dealing with the lives of Catholic men and women who have played an important part in the history of our Continent. Although most of these books concern those whose contributions were made to the discovery, exploration, and development of the United States, the series introduces young readers also to the heroes and heroines of Canada and other American countries. Great explorers, colonizers, war heroes, pioneer women, and missionaries, as well as those prominent in the fields of sport and the arts, are among those whose lives and adventures light up the pages of these books.

AMERICAN BACKGROUND BOOKS have been written by authors well qualified to deal with each period and subject. While the facts have been thoroughly researched, the authors handle their material in a way that stresses human interest and adventure and fosters pride in the American religious heritage.

"Here we have books which recognize by the dignity of their craftsmanship that our children are intelligent, reflective, well-trained readers."—*Martha C. Engler, Boston Public Library*
"Because the religious element is handled objectively, these . . . stories should be found suitable for all youngsters . . . of any or no religious denomination."—*Virginia Kirkus*
"A valuable addition to upper grade and high school libraries."
—*Catholic School Journal*

AMERICAN

BACKGROUND

BOOKS